"This book gives practical insight into becoming Christlike from the inside out and experiencing the kind of love that brings joy and contentment to oneself and to others. Randy Frazee has done a good job conveying Dallas Willard's material to students. By teaching this message to the younger generation, needed reform will happen in the church. Change in the church does not start with the board of elders—it starts in the nursery!"

DOUG FIELDS,

president, Simply Youth Ministry; author, *Purpose Driven Youth Ministry;*

student pastor, Saddleback Church

Go Ahead:

TH1NK: *about God*

about life

about others

Faith isn't just an act; it's something you live—something huge and sometimes unimaginable. By getting into the real issues in your life, TH1NK books open opportunities to talk honestly about your faith, your relationship with God and others, as well as all the things life throws at you.

Don't let other people th1nk for you . . .

TH1NK for yourself.

RENOVATION
OF THE HEART

PUTTING ON THE CHARACTER OF CHRIST

AN INTERACTIVE STUDENT EDITION

Dallas Willard and Randy Frazee

TH1NK Books
an imprint of NavPress®

THiNK
P.O. Box 35001
Colorado Springs, Colorado 80935

www.navpress.com
THiNK is an imprint of NavPress.
THiNK and the THiNK logo are registered trademarks of NavPress. Absence of ® in connection with marks of NavPress or other parties does not indicate an absence of registration of those marks.

ISBN 1-57683-730-0

Cover design by BURNKIT
Cover image by BURNKIT
Creative Team: Gabe Filkey s.c.m., Don Simpson, Nicci Jordan, Arvid Wallen, Kathy Mosier, Glynese Northam

Printed in Canada

1 2 3 4 5 6 7 8 9 10 / 09 08 07 06 05

FOR A FREE CATALOG OF
NAVPRESS BOOKS & BIBLE STUDIES,
CALL 1-800-366-7788 (USA)
OR 1-800-839-4769 (CANADA)

CONTENTS

PREFACE

It has been my great honor to rewrite *Renovation of the Heart* for students and the faithful readers of the TH1NK line of books. Bob Buford once referred to Dallas as the statue in the Parthenon of Spiritual Formation. Dallas would never say that about himself, but that is what others are saying about him. His good friend Richard Foster backs up Buford's opinion by saying that "no one has thought more carefully than Dallas Willard about the human personality and how it can be transformed into Christlikeness." I couldn't agree more. I believe Dallas is the greatest living thinker on the topic. Dallas, I pray that this student edition of *Renovation* expands your readership to an audience who desperately needs to hear what you have to say—what Christ is saying through you.

I first met Dallas in the mid-'90s. He came to Arlington, Texas, to speak at the local university. He was kind enough to give me about two hours of his time. I had read his previous works and asked him to critique the way I had applied his suggestions to the local congregation I love and serve. Everything I do as a pastor has been influenced by the careful writings and Christlike character of Dallas Willard. He has a renovated heart.

In addition to Dallas, I would also like to thank a handful of other people. I want to thank Jay and Jen Howver for recommending me to NavPress to tackle this awesome assignment. I cherish our friendship. I would like to thank the creative team at NavPress for their great talent and passion for their work and for God: Gabe Filkey, Don Simpson, Nicci Jordan, Arvid Wallen, Kathy Mosier, and Glynese Northam.

I want to thank Amy Harivson for writing all of the prayers in this book. She is truly an authentic follower of Jesus with an inspired gift. I believe in her and what God has entrusted to her. Whatever you do, don't miss the opportunity to experience these prayers.

I would also like to acknowledge Maria Garman, my personal assistant. What a dedicated follower of Christ who has been strapped with the calling to manage a person such as me. A crown awaits you in heaven for this, I'm sure.

My lovely wife, Rozanne, helped me so much with this project. She is not only the wife spoken of in Proverbs 31 but also a very talented thinker and editor. What a joy to be married to a person who truly loves God.

Finally, I want to thank my four children, Jennifer, David, Stephen, and Austin. At the writing of this book, they are twenty, seventeen, fourteen, and twelve. They are the intended audience for the TH1NK books. The entire time I rewrote the deep words of Dr. Willard, I had a picture of them on my desk. It is a gross understatement to say that they inspire me.

Randy Frazee

HOW TO USE THIS BOOK

Although you can definitely benefit from reading this book alone, it's ideal to use this interactive student guide in a group. It's a good idea to include parents and other adults in your group, but at a minimum, invite your youth leader to participate. I stress the presence of adults because, as author Quentin Schultze says, "How are youth going to mature except by contact with adults?"[1]

The book is divided into ten main parts, each with several chapters. You will find as you read that the chapters will take you through a process of renovation. The early sections will introduce you to the concepts and will tend to be a little more interactive in nature. The later sections will probe more deeply into each concept and will therefore have longer chapters. I urge you to take advantage of the various features of this student edition:

- **Read Out Loud:** I encourage you to read the chapters out loud in a small group. That group can be you and your parents, a small group with your youth leader, or just a group of your friends. Many of the chapters are short to encourage you to read them in a group. Your group can decide to read the longer chapters all at once or break them up according to what works best for you.

- **Activities:** You'll encounter activities throughout the book, set apart from the rest of the text and designed to help you take what you're learning one step further by putting it into action, sometimes individually and sometimes with your group.

- **Group Prayer:** You will find a prayer at the end of each chapter that you can pray together as a group. This is simply a suggested prayer, however, so feel free to come up with your own instead if you would prefer.

- **Wrap Up:** Found at the end of each main part, this will bring together and summarize the material covered in that section. It is intended to help you review key points. Beginning with part 5, the Wrap Up will include a Personal Renovation Plan for you to complete. By the end of the book, you will have a concrete plan in place to get started on renovating your heart.

I believe you'll enjoy these features. And, as you seek God's involvement, I trust you'll experience genuine progress in the renovation of your heart.

WELCOME TO THE GREATEST ADVENTURE OF YOUR LIFE

Adventure requires courage to keep us faithful to the struggle, since by its very nature adventure means that the future is always in doubt. And just to the extent that the future is in doubt, hope is required, as there can be no adventure if we despair of our goal. Such hope does not necessarily take the form of excessive confidence; rather, it involves the simple willingness to take the next step.

—Stanley Hauerwas

At a pivotal moment in *The Matrix*, the older guide, Morpheus, tells his young friend, "Neo, sooner or later you're going to realize just as I did that there's a difference between knowing the path and walking the path."[1] Many of us find ourselves at just that crucial place—we know something about this path that Jesus is beckoning us toward, but we struggle with the daily discipline of following Him consistently.

But the fact is that there is no greater adventure in life than this adventure of following Christ and becoming like Him in all that we think, say, and do. And the adventure of personal transformation is what this book is all about. It calls for starting a revolution in the world—a revolution of the heart, a revolution that begins with us.

What is your vision for your life right now? Perhaps no one has asked you this question before, but it's likely that you have thought about it—at least now and then. Maybe right now you're just a little overwhelmed by life. Everything seems to be changing, responsibilities are growing, people are demanding things of you, and relationships are getting more complicated. Or, maybe you're bored. Nothing significant is happening; nothing really grabs your interest or your passion. You feel like you are in limbo—stuck.

On the other hand, perhaps this is a time of great difficulty for you. You may even be feeling depressed about your situation. Nothing seems to be working. You've tried a few things in the way of relationships or getting a handle on the future, but your plans have fizzled out or never really gotten off the ground. There may be conflict in your relationships with no hope of a peaceful resolution any time soon. That conflict may be with your boyfriend or girlfriend, your best friend, or even your parents.

Whatever your situation in life, do you believe that significant change is possible? You may think that good things will happen to you only when your external circumstances change. But I hope to persuade you that moving from tension, insecurity, boredom—you name it—into liveliness, confidence, and purpose begins on the inside. It begins with a "renovation of the heart." You don't have to remain stuck in old patterns and painfully familiar responses to life. And you definitely don't have to wait until you are older or have more money or more education.

Another life is possible, and you won't be all alone in finding it. Even in the most secret places of your heart where you may question your abilities or your hope for the future, you have an absolutely supportive Friend who knows you inside and out. And He's going to stick with you throughout the entire adventure of renovation.

Pause for a moment and think about what Jesus says about this new life: "Everyone who drinks this water will get thirsty again and again. Anyone who drinks the water I give will never thirst—not ever. The water I give will be an artesian spring within, gushing fountains of endless life" (John 4:13-14).

Now take in the amazing dimensions of this new life as the apostle Paul instructs: "Reach out and experience the breadth! Test its length! Plumb the depths! Rise to the heights! Live full lives, full in the fullness of God. God can do anything, you know—far more than you could ever imagine or guess or request in your wildest dreams!" (Ephesians 3:18-20).

You may feel that your life is dull or disappointing. Will you ever reach a place of satisfaction? The apostle Peter tells us what this new life in Christ produces: "an indescribable and glorious joy" (1 Peter 1:8, NRSV).

These words are not wishful thinking. Nor are they simply nice thoughts that parents say to get their children to go to church. These words are promises inspired and backed up by God Himself. They are true.

If you are excited about this renovation in your life, you likely have some questions: What is the pathway to this experience? How can I keep drinking the living water of God's kingdom and breathing its fresh air? Well, there is a lot I want to tell you, but for right now, let me give you two important things you must know:

1. This new life involves a renovation of the heart—a sort of *Trading Spaces*—in which Christ comes in and rearranges the character and priorities of our inner lives.

2. This new life involves taking one small step at a time. In other words, it doesn't happen overnight, but each step you are invited to take is within your grasp. God will help you from beginning to end.

This awesome way of life doesn't require equipment, programs, talents, or even money. (You might be saying, "Good thing, because I don't have any money.") It just requires faithfulness to a doable process that God has marked out in the Bible, the pattern of how He wants to renovate our hearts so we can become like Jesus. It's a path anyone can walk.

Has anyone ever experienced it? Yes, absolutely. There have been many people throughout the ages and even many today. But the unfortunate fact is that most Christians don't experience this renovation today because they haven't really tried it or they gave up too soon.

Here's a good reminder: God has a vision for you. He says, "I know what I'm doing. I have it all planned out—plans to take care of you, not abandon you, plans to give you the future you hope for" (Jeremiah 29:11). He wants you to be one of His people who take the "living water plunge," to live a life you can't even imagine right now, to experience an indescribable joy. God is giving you—yes, you (don't ever underestimate God's love and knowledge of you)—a personal invitation to a life full of vision. You're probably going to want to respond.

GROUP PRAYER: *Dear God, we realize that You have a vision for our lives—a vision for each one of us. We acknowledge that You know each of us intimately and You love us. We want to respond to You today and tell You, "We're in!" All we know is that You want to renovate our hearts and all we need to do is take one small step at a time. Show us those steps, Lord, and we will follow.*

PART 1
LESSONS ON RENOVATING
THE HEART

Keep vigilant watch over your heart;
that's where life starts. (Proverbs 4:23)

THINK ABOUT IT: Today, reality TV has taken the world by storm. One of the most successful reality TV programs has been *American Idol.* People from all over the country demonstrate their musical talent (or lack thereof) in front of three judges—Simon, Paula, and Randy—and in front of the entire world in hopes of becoming the next American idol. We know that Jesus doesn't judge by the same standards as *American Idol,* but what criteria *does* He use to judge us?

Psychologists say that our character, which is the content of our hearts, is formed by the time we are five years old. This means that whether you are sixteen or twenty-six, your heart has already been set. That's not to say change can't happen, but it means that deep and lasting change will take genuine effort one step at a time.

Our hearts are shaped by the experiences we have lived through and the choices we have made in our pasts. The world we now live in is a world we have created together by the particular choices we've made.

You may ask, "Do you mean to say that the disasters that fill the human scene are not imposed upon us from someone or something outside ourselves? They don't just happen to us?"

Yes, that is what I mean. In today's world, car wrecks, war, and violence—including the Columbine tragedy, 9/11, and even what you will see on the news tonight if you care or dare to watch it—are almost totally the outcome of human choice. And because all these choices come from the heart as Proverbs 4:23 tells us, the *renovation of the heart* becomes the central issue and the only hope of a different world.

Sometimes other people make choices that hurt you. Maybe a friend has talked behind your back, you've just moved and have to go to a new school and make all new friends, or your family has experienced a tragedy of some kind.

The situation you find yourself in may be very painful, and the comfort of friends might mean a lot to you right now. But the key to healing and hope for the future is how you respond to what has happened to you. And that response will come from your heart according to how it has been formed. Think about this: A carefully cultivated heart will, with God's help, foresee, forestall, or transform a painful situation. But when faced with tragedy, a heart that has not been cultivated in this way will probably just helplessly ask, "Why?"

In this section of the book, you will be introduced to six lessons for renovating the heart. This will help you develop a good foundation for the rest of the book.

GROUP PRAYER: *Loving God, give us eyes to look deep inside our hearts, for that is where life begins. Take everything in us that needs changing. Transform our hearts so that we can respond to every situation in a way that reflects Your love. Come renovate our hearts, Lord. We're ready!*

CHAPTER 1

RENOVATING THE HEART, LESSON 1

LESSON 1: JESUS' STRATEGY IS UNIQUE

HE WORKS FROM THE INSIDE OUT

> revolution \re-və-'lü-shən\ n: *a fundamental change in the way of thinking about or visualizing something: a change of paradigm*[1]

The American Revolution was a bloody war in our country's history that supposedly shaped many of the written values and beliefs of our nation. Yet you would probably agree with me that many Americans today don't know what these values and beliefs are, don't care, or don't really live them out in their lives. Though this revolution was influential at the time, the impact has lost steam in the years since.

Consider also the little girl who threw a temper tantrum because she was not getting her way. Her mother stepped in and demanded that she sit down and take a time-out. The little girl refused. The mother finally threatened to spank her bottom, and the girl sat down. After she sat down, she folded her arms, let out a big rush of air, and said, "I may be sitting down on the outside, but I am standing up on the inside." A revolution in this little girl's heart obviously did not occur.

Jesus is a revolutionary. He has a vision and a plan to change the world. But, unlike the two examples above, Jesus understands our nature and therefore has a different strategy for encouraging our behaviors to match our hearts. He knows we live from the heart and make every choice from the heart. Therefore, His revolution targets the renovation of our hearts' values, beliefs, and practices. In the kind of world Jesus wants to bring into being, the tragedy of 9/11 would not happen, not because outside authorities would prevent it, but because people would *choose* to live differently—from the heart.

This is why Jesus had no intent to overthrow the Roman government of His time. He told His accusers that He was not interested in Caesar's job because His kingdom was going to be totally different. His kingdom was and is spiritual. His base of operations would not be Rome or the Oval Office but our hearts. Through our ongoing relationships with Him and with other Christ-followers, He begins to reform our hearts' beliefs, ideals, feelings, and habits of choice. This progressive internal change governs our actions, bodily tendencies, and relationships with others. With Jesus, righteous behavior flows from a heart governed by Him.

From the divinely renovated heart, social structures, such as government, will naturally be transformed so that "justice roll[s] down like waters, and righteousness like an ever-flowing stream" (Amos 5:24, NRSV). Such streams *cannot* flow from corrupted souls. On the flip side, a renovated heart will not cooperate or participate with public streams of unrighteousness. What does that mean? In school there's a great deal of public pressure from fellow students and instructors to think or act in a way that is inappropriate. A renovated heart will not bow down to this pressure and participate in words or acts that are unrighteous, even if it means being rejected.

THINK ABOUT THIS: There was a time in America when it was illegal to have an abortion, but women still aborted babies because they thought it was their "right." Now abortion is not only considered a right but is also legal. This has greatly increased the number of abortions that women are having—an estimated three million a year. There is growing public pressure to consider someone who doesn't believe in the right to abortion uneducated and narrow-minded. One strategy of pro-life advocates is to get the law reversed. This would be a good thing. Another is to counsel unmarried pregnant women against abortion and in favor of adoption. But one way or another, as followers of Christ whose hearts are under construction, we'll surely struggle over the important issue of abortion. The best strategy is a renovation of the heart, not just a reversal of the law. Discuss in your group why a reversal of the law is not enough to cause a revolution.

Those of us who have received Christ into our hearts are being instructed by Him so that we may "be blameless and harmless, children of God, faultless in the midst of a twisted and misguided generation, from within which they shine as lights in the world, lifting up a word of life" (Philippians 2:15-16, PAR). This is God's vision for you and for His church. The church is His primary agent of change to bring about His kingdom—not by imposing morality on others from the outside but through the power of renovated hearts, one person at a time.

GROUP PRAYER: *Lord, change us from the inside out. Instruct us so that we can be Your righteous children and be able to change the direction of our misguided generation. We want to shine like lights in this dark world. Cause a revolution in our hearts!*

CHAPTER 2

RENOVATING THE HEART, LESSONS 2–4

LESSON 2: FACE THE FACTS

WHAT'S ON THE INSIDE SHOWS UP ON THE OUTSIDE

By the age of forty everyone has the face they deserve.
—Oscar Wilde, author (1854–1900)

Over time, our faces take on the outward expression of what is inside us. If we continually wear a scowl or if our mouths naturally curve down, or if we have lines of stress stamped on our foreheads, it may indicate that we have chosen to allow ourselves to be angry or stressed about life. Likewise, if our mouths naturally curve upward, it may mean we have chosen to face life with a positive attitude. Of course, this is not always a good indicator as part of this may be the genetic structure of our faces. But the next time you are at the mall, without being judgmental or mean, look at the faces of people over forty and consider what their facial structures tell you.

In the quote above, Oscar Wilde is saying that our faces reflect the choices we have made over the years. As we have already seen, these choices come from our hearts. Here's the dilemma: We cannot see the deep, inner dimensions of our hearts. We cannot always know why we think or feel a certain way or why we choose to do what we do. The heart is very complicated and devious at times. However, in order to renovate our hearts, there must be a change. This is where God comes in and helps. He sees our hearts in full color. That is why the psalmist cries out,

Investigate my life, O God,
  find out everything about me;
Cross-examine and test me,
    get a clear picture of what I'm about. (Psalm 139:23)

Look in the mirror at your own face. This is the face that God has given you. There are things that will most likely go away, like acne. There are also lines and other features that are yet to be etched on your face. Now, count how many years you have until you reach forty. Every day you live, you make choices that will shape your face. Today, plastic surgery may be able to change the shape of our faces for a while, but it can't change the shape of our hearts. Only Christ can do that. So we cry out to Him for help. We must face this fact if we want to live out Christ's vision for us.

LOOK DEEPLY: As you're looking in the mirror, consider your face. Look deeply, from your face to your eyes to your inner being. Do you think your face accurately represents who you are on the inside? Are there smile lines? Forehead wrinkles? What do your eyes say? As you look at the reflection of your inner being, consider areas of your life that you want to renovate.

LESSON 3: SCIENCE CLASS MISSES THE HEART

THE SPIRITUAL LIFE IS THE CENTER OF LIFE

science \'sī-ən(t)s\ **n:** *such knowledge or such a system of knowledge concerned with the physical world and its phenomena*[1]

On a scale of 1 to 10 (with 10 being the best), how would you rate science class? Unless I'm off, you probably would give it a 5 or below.

Of course, if you are a future doctor or scientist, you probably really dig science class. Science deals with the physical world—things we can see, smell, touch, hear, and taste. And Jesus created everything in the physical world that gives science teachers something to talk about. Because Jesus created it, it is good.

However, Jesus says science misses the heart. When did He say this? Near the beginning of His ministry, He said, "It takes more than bread to stay alive" (Matthew 4:4). Jesus was saying that if we want to live, it takes more than eating physical bread. We must take in the bread that feeds the soul. This *spiritual* bread guides how we think and feel, what we do and why, and what kind of character we will have. What is this spiritual bread? Or better, *who* is this spiritual bread? Jesus is the Bread of Life (see John 6:35). If we constantly feast ourselves on the presence of Christ, we can live the life of the renovated heart.

P.S.: Notice that Jesus doesn't disregard the physical world. We still have to feed our bodies. And it's not the best idea to tell your parents that you didn't do your science homework because Jesus doesn't think it's important. You might end up with a punishment that can be felt in the physical world!

LESSON 4: JESUS AND OPRAH ARE NOT TALKING ABOUT THE SAME THING

RENOVATION DOESN'T COME FROM HUMAN EFFORT APART FROM GOD

Pick up a copy of a popular magazine at the checkout counter of the grocery store or watch a few shows of *Oprah*, and you will probably see a good portion of space or time dedicated to how the physical world looks, especially our bodies. However, a section of these magazine issues and TV episodes are focused on the development of a high-quality inner life. Almost every tip offered suggests that we have the power within ourselves to make positive changes apart from God.

Jesus would say this is attempting to accomplish the right thing (the transformation of the inner life, the heart) with the wrong tool (human ability). Consider what Paul said in the Bible:

> Only crazy people would think they could complete by their own efforts what was begun by God. If you weren't smart enough or strong enough to begin it, how do you suppose you could perfect it? Did you go through this whole painful learning process for nothing? It is not yet a total loss, but it certainly will be if you keep this up! (Galatians 3:3-4)

Here's the deal: If we want to experience a genuine renovation of the heart, we can't do it with our own strength. We need God's help. Jesus and Oprah are not talking about the same thing.

GROUP PRAYER: *Dear God, would You do an examination of our hearts? Ask us tough questions until the truth of who we really are is revealed. Help us to see beyond knowledge and human effort. Satisfy our hearts with the Bread of Life. We need Your strength to bring about real changes within us.*

CHAPTER 3

RENOVATING THE HEART, LESSONS 5-6

LESSON 5: WHO ARE YOU WEARING?

RENOVATION INVOLVES DRESSING OUR HEARTS IN CHRIST

Do you know how I feel right now, and will feel until Christ's life becomes visible in your lives? (Galatians 4:19)

How students dress is a big deal. As I write this book, Abercrombie & Fitch and Urban Outfitters are hot. But this will change quickly. Trends always do. It's interesting that the Bible tells us that as Christians we should pay attention to more than just our clothes. In fact, it actually says, "Dress yourselves in Christ" (Romans 13:14).

Many people throughout the ages have tried to dress like Christ outwardly without an inward transformation first. They dress themselves in behaviors they call Christian, and yet their hearts do not have the connection with Christ that really matters. This outward spiritual dress takes on many styles depending on when and where the person lives. They might wear a robe and sandals. They might think it means that men keep their hair short and girls wear dresses that go well below their knees. Maybe it is someone who wears a W.W.J.D. bracelet or puts a Christian fish decal on his car. These things are not bad in and of themselves. However, you can do all these things and still never experience what it really means to dress in Christ.

STOP AND THINK ABOUT IT: Are you beginning to see that real change of character can't be added to the outside of a person? When Paul talks about dressing ourselves in Christ, where does that wardrobe change begin? What will you wear?

When the Bible talks about clothing ourselves in Christ, it is speaking about spiritual formation. What is spiritual formation? This term refers to the Spirit-driven process of forming the inner part of the human self in such a way that it becomes like the inner being of Christ Himself. As this happens, our outer lives—our spiritual clothing, in other words—become a natural expression of the teaching and character of Jesus because we start to look like Him on the inside.

So if you are really serious about this whole renovation thing, it doesn't matter if you wear Abercrombie & Fitch or the generic Wal-Mart brand. If you are becoming like Christ on the inside, it will bleed through whatever you are wearing on the outside and show your true colors—that you are undeniably a child of Jesus.

LESSON 6: JESUS' WAY IS EASIER

RENOVATION FOCUSES ON WHO WE ARE IN OUR HEARTS, NOT ON OUR HARD WORK TO ACT LIKE JESUS ON THE OUTSIDE

Let's say a new student shows up on your campus in the middle of the year. Friendship circles are already established. To make matters worse for this student, she is different. She is not pretty; she dresses differently and comes from a poor family.

Your classmates start making fun of her behind her back. You know it is only a matter of time before they do this to her face. The thing is, you know they are doing this to build up their own weak identities. You know this because you have done it yourself from time to time.

You decide to reach out and love this student. You really don't care about her that much; you just think it's the Christian thing to do. You even risk being ridiculed and rejected by students who currently accept you. This favored position of acceptance was a tough thing to earn, and now you are jeopardizing it.

Two things happen. First, the other students (some of them your friends) start whispering negative things about you. Second, what you didn't expect was the difficulty of loving the new girl. She appreciates what you are doing, but she is a little weird, and it turns out that she isn't much fun to be around. You feel you have made a mistake. You are angry with your friends, the new student, even yourself. You feel that the future is hopeless—all because you tried to do the right thing and love someone.

While we should always do the best we can in our outward actions, if we focus only on the outward element, we will end up in defeat. This is because we are not in control of all the outer factors. They move on us. They usually turn out to be different from what we expected.

What we will discover in the chapters to come, however, is that if we focus on our inner characters and our relationships with Christ, we will be able to weather any downturn in fortune that life may throw at us. He will be the source of our love.

So, trying to *act* loving on our own doesn't go deep enough and therefore often fails. Instead, it is love itself—not just loving behavior—that must drive our actions. It must come from our hearts. We must begin with a genuine inner readiness and longing to secure the good of others. Jesus' strategy begins with who we are, not with what we do or how we act.

Trying to love someone is hard, isn't it? Something radically new has to take place in our hearts for true love to flow from us. We have to become loving on the inside before we'll be successful in *acts* of love on the outside in real relationships. This is the revolutionary adventure we will be pursuing in this book.

Have you tried loving others and experienced the difficulty of sticking with it? Jesus' way is easier. Here's what Jesus says about the life He offers you:

> *"Are you tired? Worn out? Burned out on religion? Come to me. Get away with me and you'll recover your life. I'll show you how to take a real rest. Walk with me and work with me—watch how I do it. Learn the unforced rhythms of grace. I won't lay anything heavy or ill-fitting on you. Keep company with me and you'll learn to live freely and lightly."* (Matthew 11:28-30)

MOVIE RENTAL NIGHT: Rent *A Walk to Remember* (rated PG-13), starring Mandy Moore. Talk with your group about how you see the principles from all six lessons in chapters 1–3 expressed in this movie. Do you think you would have been as patient as Mandy? How do you think you would have behaved in her situation? Who is she wearing?

GROUP PRAYER: *Dear Lord, help us to realize that what matters is Jesus in our hearts. We want Your Spirit to change the way our hearts are dressed. We want to become people who look like Jesus and who really live like Him, too.*

WRAP UP

Let's review the principles from chapters 1–3.

CHAPTER 1: LESSON 1

• Jesus' strategy is unique—He works from the inside out.

CHAPTER 2: LESSONS 2–4

• Face the facts—What's on the inside shows up on the outside.
• Science class misses the heart—The spiritual life is the center of life.
• Jesus and Oprah are not talking about the same thing—Renovation doesn't come from human effort apart from God.

CHAPTER 3: LESSONS 5–6

• Who are you wearing?—Renovation involves dressing our hearts in Christ.
• Jesus' way is easier—Renovation focuses on who we are in our hearts, not on our hard work to act like Jesus on the outside.

THINK AGAIN: Go back to the *American Idol* case study on page 16. In light of what you have read about renovating the heart in these six lessons, does Jesus judge differently than you expected?

GROUP PRAYER: *God, turn us inside out. Give us Your strength and Your life so we can be in the middle of the big thing You are doing in our world. Put the Jesus label on our hearts. Change our focus from doing to being. We are part of the renovation revolution!*

PART 2
RENOVATING THE PARTS OF ME

CAUSE AND EFFECT: Most people are familiar with the horror that took place at Columbine High School in Littleton, Colorado, on April 20, 1999. Eric Harris, eighteen, and Dylan Klebold, seventeen, came to school with guns and opened fire on students and faculty. When it was all over, they had killed thirteen people and wounded twenty-three. No one will know precisely why they did what they did because they then turned the guns on themselves and took their own lives. However, there has been a great deal of speculation about why they did it. What do you think could possibly have motivated them to commit this atrocious act?

Rank the options below from the most likely cause (1) to the least likely (9):

_____ Upbringing by parents

_____ Company they kept

_____ Medications they were taking (Prozac)

_____ Movies, music, and other media influences

_____ Judas factor—they were destined to do it

_____ A choice made from their hearts

_____ Their gender—boys are prone to this kind of violence

_____ Peer pressure or a dare

_____ Taunting from perceived enemies at school (other teen groups, teachers)

A certain expert stood up to check [Jesus] out, saying: "Teacher, what shall I do to receive eternal life?"

Jesus responded, "What does the law say? How do you read it?"

And he answered: "YOU SHALL LOVE THE LORD YOUR GOD WITH ALL YOUR HEART, AND WITH ALL YOUR SOUL, AND WITH ALL YOUR STRENGTH, AND WITH ALL YOUR MIND; AND YOUR NEIGHBOR AS YOURSELF."

And Jesus said, "Well, there you have your answer. Do that and you will live." (Luke 10:25-28, PAR)

Several years ago, *Reader's Digest* ran some helpful articles on the various parts of the body: the ears, the lungs, the feet, the stomach—you get the idea. The aim of the articles was to educate readers on how to better care for their physical health.

Because you have probably taken classes on health and anatomy, you know that the human body is a complex machine to understand. So, to make the articles less intimidating, the authors gave them fun titles such as, "I'm Joe's Liver" (or lung, or foot, and so on). Each article described that particular part and then explained its role in the body as a whole.

Caring for your spiritual life can also be very complicated and hard to understand. The aim of part 2 is to introduce you to the five major parts of human nature and the role each plays in our spiritual formation in such a way that it is fun and not too intimidating. Jesus identified the five parts in His response to the lawyer in Luke 10:25-28: heart, soul, strength (body), mind, and neighbor (social dimension).

As you read this section of the book, think about Eric and Dylan's situation at Columbine. While we cannot truly know their hearts like God can, we can gain some insight on why people do good things and bad things by looking deeper into the teaching of Jesus. What Eric and Dylan did cannot be undone. But we can learn from their experience. I think we'll see in the chapters to come that the Columbine incident could have been prevented by paying attention to Jesus' double commandment of love as recorded in Luke 10:25-28, which addresses all the dimensions of our human nature.

GROUP PRAYER: *Dear God, help us to understand our hearts. We want to love You with all that we are. Teach us how to love You with our hearts, souls, strength, and minds. And God, help us to learn to love others, too. Renovate our every part!*

CHAPTER 4

DEFINING THE PARTS OF ME, PART 1

Just as *Reader's Digest* attributed parts of the body to "Joe," let's do the same for our souls, which encompass all the parts of our bodies. So how did God wire Joe? Well, as we saw in the last few pages, Jesus created our friend Joe with five parts that all work together to influence the outcome of Joe's life. The following diagram gives us a picture of Joe's entire self. It lets us see what's really going on in Joe's spiritual life.

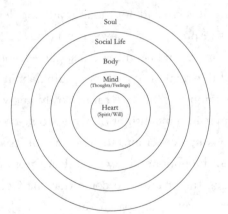

Just as Jesus said, Joe is made up of five parts. Let's lay out a simple definition of each part in this chapter. Then in the next chapter, we will look at how they work together.

"I'M JOE'S HEART"

The heart is at the center because it is the boss of our lives, the CEO, the BMOC (Big Man on Campus). It is where we make choices. It is where we say, "Yes," "No," "I don't care," or "I care." It is where we choose good or evil. It is the place where sin is chosen. The Bible also refers to the heart as the "spirit" or the "will." While other parts of our lives influence the heart, it is the heart that ultimately chooses.

HEART ISSUES: Our hearts are pulled in many directions, often several times a day. Think for a moment about the ways in which your heart has been tugged in the last few days. Have you thought about or received invitations to participate in activities that would press the limits of your sense of right and wrong? How have you reacted to these pressures?

"I'M JOE'S MIND"

Joe also has a mind that works night and day. It's separate from his heart, but it constantly tries to make suggestions to his heart about directions to take. Joe's mind is made up of two sections: thoughts and feelings.

THOUGHTS

Joe's mind enables him to think about many things and consider their relationship to other things. It is here that Joe imagines and perceives. For example, a long time ago people use to *think* the earth was flat. Today, with the same kind of mind but more information, people *think* the earth is round. The mind may be right or wrong about what it perceives, but it is the mind that ponders things.

THINK ABOUT THIS: This exercise will take at least two people; three is ideal. The goal is to determine with your God-given mind the identity and situation of the person described in the following sentence:

"Relentlessly pursued by an opposing army, he suddenly found that he had nowhere to run or hide."[1]

One of you needs to find and keep the answer privately (the answer is recorded at the end of the chapter on page 36), and the other person or persons need to ask only yes-or-no questions to figure out the riddle.

FEELINGS

Joe's mind not only thinks but also feels. His mind determines how he *feels* about what he *thinks*. Joe's mind may completely understand something, but he may have a different feeling about it than everyone else. He can like or dislike it, agree or disagree with it, be comfortable or uncomfortable with it, care or not care about it.

THINK ABOUT AND FEEL THIS:

Going to summer school so you'll have a lighter load your senior year

- Do you understand the idea?
- How do you feel about the idea?

Being drafted into the army to defend your country

- Do you understand the idea?
- How do you feel about the idea?

GROUP PRAYER: *Father God, our hearts are the center of our lives. We want our hearts to choose You and Your ways. Renew our minds so that our thoughts and feelings choose You and Your ways, too. We want all of our decisions to make You pleased.*

ANSWER TO RIDDLE ON PAGE 35: "He was the king in a game of chess. The player's opponent had just put the player's king in checkmate. The king was not safe where he was and could not move without being captured. The game is over."[2]

CHAPTER 5

DEFINING THE PARTS OF ME, PART 2

In the last chapter I introduced you to Joe's heart and mind. In this chapter, I want to introduce you to Joe's body, social life, and soul.

"I'M JOE'S BODY"

The body is what you think it is and much more. Jesus says our bodies are our "strength" to love God and others. They are our presence in the physical and social world. Our bodies are stimulated and affected by the world around us. With our bodies we recognize others, and they recognize us. We receive our bodies from God through our parents, and these influences make us the kind of people we are.

When our hearts make a choice, it is our bodies that usually carry out that decision. For example, when our hearts decide to stay out past curfew and go over to a friend's house, it is our bodies that carry out that decision by getting into the car. When our hearts decide to read God's Word, it is our bodies that open up the Bible.

Our bodies can get us into a heap of trouble; they have a "mind of their own." Our bodies often act before we think. Even though our bodies are essentially good, not evil (because God created our bodies and called His work "good"), they are prone to sin. In the Bible, Paul often calls our bodies "the flesh." He writes, "The flesh wants what is contrary to the spirit [the heart] and the spirit what is contrary to the flesh. They are in opposition to each other, so that it is impossible for you to do what you really want" (Galatians 5:17, PAR).

But here is the good news. Just as Paul says our minds can be renewed (see Romans 12:2), so can our bodies. He says,

> *Didn't you realize that your body is a sacred place, the place of the Holy Spirit? Don't you see that you can't live however you please, squandering what God paid such a high price for? The physical part of you is not some piece of property belonging to the spiritual part of you. God owns the whole works. So let people see God in and through your body.* (1 Corinthians 6:19-20)

"I'M JOE'S SOCIAL LIFE"

God made us social beings. Some of us like big parties, while some of us prefer to hang out with one friend at a time. Either way, God has hardwired us to connect with others. Some can't get any schoolwork done because all they can think about is being with their friends. Others avoid contact with people because they don't want to feel rejected or get hurt, or maybe because they just want to be alone. But either way, our social life is very important to us. We can try to ignore it, pretending that God and people don't matter, but that strategy just won't work. The more we try to ignore our social dimension, the more we think about it.

Whether we're introverted or extroverted, there is a component in each of us that yearns for connection and calls us to relate to other people. This element is as much a part of us as our hearts, minds, and bodies. As a matter of fact, the central goal of life, according to Jesus, is to have a social life with God and others. That means a life full of love.

Studies show that infants who don't receive love and attention by their mother or others will be wounded for life and may even die. Children must bond with their mothers or with *someone* in order to take on a healthy self-identity and develop normally. Rejection, no matter one's age, is a sword thrust into the soul that has literally killed many. Numerous people have experienced rejection from their parents when they got a divorce or from a friend who betrayed or embarrassed them. The student, more than anyone, knows how important it is to have a healthy social life.

The quality of our social lives affects the other parts of our lives—our choices, our inner thoughts and feelings, how we feel about our bodies, and even our actions. Here's the bottom line: Having and maintaining a good relationship with God and others may be one of the most difficult assignments we have as human beings, but Jesus tells us it is the most important and is possible through Him. As a matter of fact, this is what the church is all about. As the church, we are Christ's body, His presence on earth today to love people in the manner He did when He was here. Now that's a life of purpose!

EXERCISING THE BODY OF CHRIST: Think of someone who feels discouraged or rejected and call or e-mail this person with a word of encouragement.

"I'M JOE'S SOUL"

The final part of Joe is his soul. The soul is the whole person. It connects all the other dimensions or parts (the heart, mind, body, and social dimension) together to form one life. Let's use an analogy, albeit a somewhat weak one, to understand this difficult concept better. The soul is like a cell phone. Here are a few of the parts:

- Phone chip (tiny card that connects the phone to the provider) = the Heart (spirit/ will)
- Circuitry (the inside "guts" of the phone that think) = the Mind (thoughts and feelings)
- Casing—each one different (the actual, physical phone; some are flip phones and some have cool covers on them) = the Body
- Cells (our connection to others) = the Social Life

In our analogy, the soul is the whole cell phone. Just as the cell phone is the whole idea, the soul is our whole idea. The soul is all parts working together. It works without thinking about it. As a matter of fact, we don't think much about it until it doesn't work.

The soul needs to be reformed as much as the other parts. The power to reform the soul comes from the heart. The heart accomplishes this mainly by redirecting the body in spiritual disciplines and other types of experiences with God's help. For example, one of the key spiritual disciplines is worship of God. When our hearts instruct our bodies to worship God, this helps to reform our souls to be like Jesus. This may seem complicated, but stay with me. We'll talk more about this later.

Now you should have a basic understanding of the five parts of our human nature. In chapter 6, we will look at how these five parts work together to make you who you really are.

GROUP PRAYER: *Lord, understanding how You made us will help us understand how to live for You. We choose to use our bodies to love and serve You. We choose to connect with You and with other people in love. We give You our whole selves—our very souls. Reform and redirect us in Your way.*

HOW THE PARTS WORK TOGETHER TO MAKE ME WHO I AM

So there you go. Now you've got an understanding of how God has made all the parts of you. But how do these parts work together?

Our actions never come from our hearts alone. Even though our hearts ultimately choose the actions we take, each action involves all the other parts of our human nature as well. As a matter of fact, most of the time our hearts make decisions because of the pressure put on them by the other parts. The drawing that follows illustrates this in our lives.

Notice how the arrows are pointing into the heart. This illustrates how these parts shape the heart to decide. Left alone with our good intentions, we will lose the battle of growing into the people Jesus envisions us to be (see the opening pages of this book—pages 11-14). This is because our hearts, or spirits, are not strong enough to overcome the pressure of the other parts. Jesus said it well: "The spirit indeed is willing, but the flesh is weak" (Matthew 26:41, NRSV). He was saying that even if our hearts want to follow what is good, right, and best, our flesh puts so

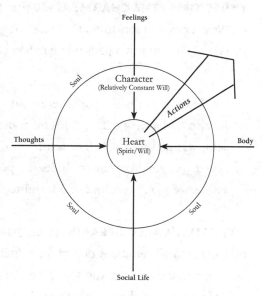

much pressure on us to do what is wrong and harmful that we will likely lose the battle. Only if the five parts of us (heart, mind, body, social life, and soul) are aligned with God do we stand a chance.

Carefully read this. Actually, read it three times in a row—slowly:

> Our actions do not change who we are but express who we are.

> Our actions do not change who we are but express who we are.

> Our actions do not change who we are but express who we are.

THREE TIMES THE CHARM: As you read this statement, how do you feel about it? What does it mean to you? Discuss in your group an example of how this statement rings true in a particular situation or area in your life.

Jesus said it best: "For where your treasure is, there your heart will be also" (Matthew 6:21, NIV). The apostle John really understood what Jesus was getting at when he wrote, "So, my dear children, don't let anyone divert you from the truth. It's the person who *acts* right who *is* right, just as we see it lived out in our righteous Messiah" (1 John 3:7).

HYPOTHETICALLY SPEAKING: Let's say hypothetically that you divulge an embarrassing secret about one of your friends to someone else. When you are confronted for doing this, you say, "I blew it!" By saying that, you imply, *I'm not the kind of person who does such a thing.* As painful as it may be, the apostle John is saying that in fact you *are* the kind of person who does such a thing—because you did it. Our actions express who we are as whole people. But take heart because this applies to the good stuff we do, too.

LIFE AWAY FROM GOD

When we do not have God in our lives controlling and directing our hearts, our hearts are at the mercy of the other parts of our nature. Once again, the other parts of our nature are the mind, the body, the social dimension, and the soul. Therefore, even though the heart knows that gossiping and breaking a confidence, for example, is wrong, it often makes the choice to do it anyway. Why? Because the rest of us is weak, and for some reason we enjoy the feeling of gossip. Really, we enjoy the feeling of sin. This is a life focused on pleasing ourselves versus getting in tune with God.

Unfortunately, even if we have a relationship with God, that relationship is often our lowest priority. In this kind of on-again, off-again faithfulness, God usually allows us to do what we want—to be happy according to our own ideas. But we miss out on the energy of His presence, the confidence of His guidance, and the joy of intimacy with Him. Pursuing happiness according to our own ideas may be sinful, and the great danger is that we may eventually drift away from Him altogether.

LIFE UNDER GOD

A life that loves God looks very different—even the complete opposite—of a life that is self-centered and moving away from Him. This more vital life begins when our hearts come alive in God, and it continues as the Holy Spirit enables us to do His will. Here is how Paul describes the difference between a life that is self-centered and one that seeks God:

> *Those who trust God's action in them find that God's Spirit is in them — living and breathing God! Obsession with self in these matters is a dead end; attention to God leads us out into the open, into a spacious, free life. Focusing on the*

self is the opposite of focusing on God. Anyone completely absorbed in self ignores God, ends up thinking more about self than God. That person ignores who God is and what he is doing. And God isn't pleased at being ignored. (Romans 8:5-8)

Once we trust Christ with our present lives and our eternal salvation, He can come in and strengthen our hearts day by day so we can choose what God wants. And here is even better news: Allowing Him to direct our hearts always leads to "a spacious, free life" (Romans 8:6). From this point of divine intervention and power, the other parts of our lives—the mind, the body, the social part, and the soul—are transformed to be obedient to God's plan. This will happen instead of our conforming to the world's plan, which always leads to death (see Romans 8:6). As you look at the drawing that follows, you will notice that God has the power to renovate your heart—and that gives you the power to direct your entire self under God's rule.

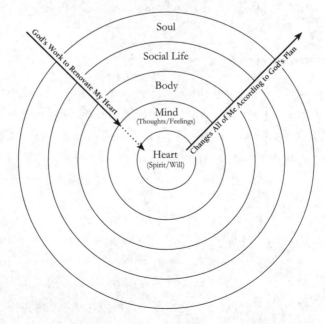

The point of this chapter: Our spiritual formation happens as all five parts of us grow up to look more and more like Christ. Such transformation cannot be accomplished by putting pressure on the heart alone and is not the result of mere human effort. We need God's power for help and His grace for the many mistakes we will make along the way.

GROUP PRAYER: *God, it's amazing. We are starting to see why our hearts need to be renovated. If we don't have the strength of Jesus Christ in our hearts, then our bodies, minds, social lives, and souls will run free, doing as they please — or as we please. Strengthen our hearts in Christ and use Your grace to change all five of our parts.*

WRAP UP

Let's review the principles from chapters 4–6.

CHAPTER 4: DEFINING THE PARTS OF ME, PART 1

• The Heart—the part where all decisions are made
• The Mind—the part that thinks and feels

CHAPTER 5: DEFINING THE PARTS OF ME, PART 2

• The Body—the physical part with all its senses
• The Social Life—the part that is hardwired to connect with others
• The Soul—the part that connects the other four parts together

CHAPTER 6: HOW THE PARTS WORK TOGETHER TO MAKE ME WHO I AM

• Life Away from God—When we don't have God in our lives controlling and directing our hearts, our hearts are at the mercy of the other parts of our nature.
• Life Under God—When we do have God in our lives controlling and directing our hearts, our hearts transform the other parts of our nature.

RETHINKING CAUSE AND EFFECT: We've looked at the conditions of lives that reject God and are self-centered, and we've looked at lives that are constantly moving toward God. Go back to the Columbine High School case study on page 30 and discuss your rankings in light of what you have read. Apply what you now understand about the five parts of people that need renovating and how they work together to produce a transformed life.

GROUP PRAYER: *God, we're IN! Turn us inside out. Give us Your strength and Your life so we can be in the middle of the big thing You are doing in our world. Put the Jesus label on our hearts. Change our focus from doing to being. We are part of the renovation revolution!*

PART 3
CHOOSE ONE: SELF-WORSHIP OR SELF-DENIAL

"Self-help is no help at all. Self-sacrifice is the way, my way, to finding yourself, your true self. What kind of deal is it to get everything you want but lose yourself? What could you ever trade your soul for?" (Matthew 16:25-26)

THE CASE OF THE STOLEN BOYFRIEND: Let's say you have a friend who stole your boyfriend away from you (if you are male, say it's your girlfriend). This leaves you feeling depressed and betrayed. Now, six months later, this girl is in big trouble and wants your help. She is failing a class that will keep her from graduating on time. This happens to be a class you are acing. She picks up the phone and gives you a call for help. There's probably a huge part of you that wants to entirely reject this girl—to laugh in her face. Or perhaps you can kindly agree to meet with her but then give her all the wrong information. What would you do?

Growing older doesn't mean that one automatically grows up, does it? The renovation of the heart doesn't take place by simply showing up for the game of life. Some of us right now are making destructive choices, but we can't see how they are going to take us down. Some of us have made destructive choices in the past, and we're now suffering the deep consequences of these actions. No one needs to tell us how awful it all is.

Perhaps there is someone in your life who has made a destructive choice, and it has hurt you—like in the case study you just read. Maybe your parents got a divorce. Possibly your parents are in the heavy-fighting stage that might end in divorce, and it scares you. Maybe you had a good friend who died from driving while drunk or from a drug overdose.

Why do people make these poor choices? Why do we? That is the focus of this part of the book. We will see that there are two possible paths to take. The first path is the one we all start off on and the one most of us stay on throughout our life. It is called *self-worship* or "the path to radical ruin." The second path is the narrow path that Jesus made available to all who trust Him. It is the path of *self-denial* or "the path to radical goodness."

In chapters 7 and 8 we will look at the path of *self-worship* and how it leads to destruction and ruin in our lives. In chapters 9 and 10 we will look at the path of *self-denial* and how it leads to the reconstruction of our lives toward radical goodness.

Here's the deal: Jesus is offering us a life of radical goodness. It is not some pie-in-the-sky sales pitch that you see on television. It is a real offer. No one else in your life can choose the path of self-denial for you. But you can, and I hope you will.

GROUP PRAYER: *Lord God, we know that only You offer a life of radical goodness. Show us how to turn from self-worship and self-help so that we can choose self-denial and self-sacrifice. We want to learn from Jesus' example. We know this is the best path.*

CHAPTER 7

SELF-WORSHIP: THE PATH TO
RADICAL RUIN, PART 1

> GOD sticks his head out of heaven.
>   He looks around.
> He's looking for someone not stupid —
>   one man, even, God-expectant,
>   just one God-ready woman.
>
> He comes up empty. A string
>   of zeros. Useless, unshepherded
> Sheep, taking turns pretending
>   to be Shepherd. (Psalm 14:2-3)

All of our parts are ruined—our hearts, our minds, our bodies, our social lives, and our souls. The thing is, we must see and acknowledge this ruin before we can understand that we will be delivered. The following drawing depicts our damaged selves.

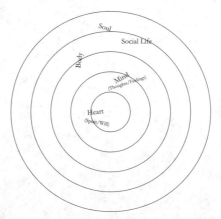

We all must see our ruin and tally the damage before we can start on the path of renovation. We must start from where we really are. That is what we are going to do in this chapter.

Here is a very important point. Just because we are ruined doesn't mean that we are worthless. As a matter of fact, it is precisely our greatness as humans that makes our ruin such a huge shame. If we were insignificant, our ruin would not be so horrifying.

G. K. Chesterton once said that the hardest thing to accept in the Christian religion is the great value it places upon the individual soul. This explains why even in its ruined condition, a human being is something God regards as immensely worth saving. Sin does not make us worthless; it just makes us lost. And in this condition the human soul is still capable of great strength, dignity, heartbreaking beauty, and goodness. As a matter of fact, some see this beauty and do not wish to deal with our ruined condition. Denial is the primary device people use to deal with their own wrongness and ruin. But not us, not today. We are going to look at the truth and deal with it. Only in that way can we be restored to the condition and place of purpose God desires.

The Bible teaches us that we are all born on a path that leads away from God. This is where we all start. And because we are not convinced there is an alternative, we continue walking down that path—a path that always leads to destruction. Without God in our lives to shed light on a better path, most people journey down the path as though it is the only option. Each step we take moves us further down that path of hopelessness, making it harder and harder to find our way out. Each step we take progressively ruins the five parts of our person, beginning with the heart and ending with the soul. That's why Jesus said, "What kind of deal is it to get everything you want but lose yourself? What could you ever trade your soul for?" (Matthew 16:26).

1. Heart Ruin: Our ruin begins when our hearts reject God's thoughts.

Our slide into utter soul corruption begins with our hearts turning our minds away from God. Our hearts reject the very thought of God being in charge. Humans have always known there is a God. We have some degree of understanding of who He is and what He is like. Romans 1:19-20 explains this clearly: "The basic reality of God is plain enough. Open your eyes and there it is! By taking a long and thoughtful look at what God has created, people have always been able to see what their eyes as such can't see: eternal power, for instance, and the mystery of his divine being. So nobody has a good excuse." Though we have this knowledge of Him, we are not pleased that He should have the central place in our universe merely because He is God. And this is the key to understanding humanity's present condition. As Saint Augustine saw clearly, God being God offends human pride. If God is running the universe and has first claim on our lives, guess who *isn't* running the universe and does not get to have things as they please? Me and you. Because that bugs most people (usually subconsciously), they make a choice in their hearts to start down the path away from God.

Maybe you know of a family in which someone struggles with alcohol. Maybe it is your own family. This is major-time ruin. The historian of Alcoholics Anonymous, Ernest Kurtz, interestingly titled his book *Not-God*. He said he did this because the determination to take the place of God is the greatest challenge an alcoholic must face. To come to terms with the fact that they will never be able to steal the role of God, alcoholics must recognize their helplessness and surrender to the Higher Power. The founders of this great program explained that addicts have to quit playing God and allow God Himself to be God in their lives. This requires surrender every moment of every day.

2. Mind Ruin: After we toss God out of our hearts, our minds try to convince us that we are god—the center of the universe—and that life is all about us.

The path starts with heart ruin and then moves to our minds—our feelings and our thoughts. When the fundamental truth about God's existence and His demand on our lives is put out of our hearts, our minds become dysfunctional. They devise amazing ways of justifying the basic falsehood that man is god. And, without really calling ourselves god, we act like it, making ourselves the center of the universe. Everything is about us. The fundamental pride of putting oneself at the center is the hinge upon which the entire world of the ruined self turns. We might do acts of goodness or kindness, but the bottom line is our needs, wants, and rights. And we don't have a problem with this way of living because our hearts have now begun feeding off the false justifications of the mind. It is not long before our whole selves become involved in a cycle of deception.

SELF-AWARENESS: If self-worship leads to radical ruin, discuss what you think self-esteem's role is in living a renovated life.

GROUP PRAYER: *Dear God, every part of us is damaged goods—but not worthless. Yet our hearts and minds still want us to be the center of the universe! Speak to our hearts and teach us so that we can begin to use our minds to honor You as Lord of all. We want to be on the path that moves us toward You.*

CHAPTER 8

SELF-WORSHIP: THE PATH TO RADICAL RUIN, PART 2

In chapter 7, we looked at the first two steps on the path to radical ruin:

1. Heart Ruin: Our ruin begins when our hearts reject God's thoughts.

2. Mind Ruin: After we toss God out of our hearts, our minds try to convince us that we are god—the center of the universe—and that life is all about us.

In this chapter, we will look at the next steps along the path of self-worship and their consequences in our lives.

3. Emotional Ruin: Our feelings soon follow along the path of chaos. Once our minds are committed to self-preservation and getting their way, we take the third step down the path of destruction—our feelings get involved. This explains why there is so much conflict among friends. Eventually, someone's feelings get hurt because people are not fully devoted to their friends' happiness. Once we are on this path, we can always expect conflict and strife to arise.

Maybe our minds believe we would be happier if we owned really expensive designer clothes. However, the hunger doesn't stop there. Our feelings quickly get locked into the idea. We feel passionate about it and will do whatever it takes to get those clothes. Some people spend all the money they have. Others even go so far as to steal. And by the way, it isn't much different for adults who are rushing down this path, except that the toys that make adults emotionally happy are often more expensive.

4. Body Ruin: When we don't worship God, we worship our bodies. The fourth step along the path of self-worship is something students are bombarded with—the pressure for body worship. Just go into a store and look at the magazine rack that markets to teenagers. The covers tell it all: "It is all about me, and the most important things about me are how I look, what others think of me, and how much pleasure my body receives."

At this point on the path, sensuality becomes central. The human body takes over as the primary area of pleasure for the person who does not live honestly and interactively with God. The mirror is the enemy to the person on this path. The goal is to look a certain way: tan, thin, and muscular. Achieving this body takes a great deal of work—tanning in tanning beds, exercising the "abs" and "buns" daily, keeping up with the latest styles. Today, if we can't work to get our bodies to look a certain way, we can usually pay for it with plastic surgery. If we are able to achieve the body that people long to have, then we show it off. If we turn on the TV to almost any channel, we will see "successful" examples of this trend.

WORKING OUT YOUR IMAGE: The next time you work out, spend time with God beforehand. Pray about your motivation and ask Him to give you a healthy, godly image of yourself as you maintain your physical health. Be sensitive to His leading. Who knows . . . He may ask you to *not* work out that day and spend more time with Him instead.

Although body worship includes anything that makes our bodies feel good (such as alcohol, eating, and drugs), sex is the biggest because it usually gives the greatest "kick." This way of thinking says, "Sex, or free love, is not wrong if we are God. After all, what we as God want is to feel good." A close second to the craze of free sex is violence.

For some reason, our bodies are stimulated by violence. Humans have always craved violence, from the Roman Colosseum to bullfights to today's high-tech video games. Just think of this: A movie gets an R rating by the amount of sex and violence it shows—and this is what we want to see.

But as you have probably already noticed, the body is also the primary source for terror, torture, and death. Sensuality *cannot* be fully satisfied, so we always have to up the ante. That is partly because the effect of engaging in sensual practices is deadened feelings. This awakens the relentless drive, the desperate need, to simply *feel*—to feel *something*. The further we step down the path, the closer we come to the destruction this way of life brings—sexually transmitted diseases, unwanted pregnancies, abortions, eating disorders, and scars from plastic surgery.

5. Soul Ruin: Our focus on ourselves leads us to become the kind of people for whom "away from God" is the only place we comfortably belong.

Self-worship has a destination. The condition is *lostness*. Lost persons, in Christian terms, are precisely the ones who mistake their own person for God. Because they are lost, they end up in the wrong place—namely, hell.

No one chooses to go to hell—or even to be the kind of person who belongs there. But our orientation toward self leads us to become the kind of person for whom "away from God" is the only place we are "at home." In the end, it is a place we choose for ourselves by choosing not to come in humility before God and accept who He is. Whether or not God's will is infinitely flexible, the human will is not. There are limits beyond which it cannot turn back and repent. Hell is not an "oops!" or a slip. One does not miss heaven by a hair but by *constant effort to avoid and escape God*. This is seen as an "in your face" kind of defiance in the Bible:

Since they didn't bother to acknowledge God, God quit bothering them and let them run loose. And then all hell broke loose: rampant evil, grabbing and grasping, vicious backstabbing. They made life hell on earth with their envy, wanton killing, bickering, and cheating. Look at them: mean-spirited, venomous, fork-tongued God-bashers. Bullies, swaggerers, insufferable windbags! They keep inventing new ways of wrecking lives. They ditch their parents when they get in the way. Stupid, slimy, cruel, cold-blooded. And it's not as if they don't know better. They know perfectly well they're spitting in God's face. And they don't care—worse, they hand out prizes to those who do the worst things best! (Romans 1:28-32)

Pretty depressing, huh? If you choose to take this path of self-worship, be prepared to be really depressed. There is another path, however, that has been made available in Christ. In the next chapter, you will be introduced to the path that leads to radical goodness.

GROUP PRAYER: *Father God, we struggle with feelings that seem crazy and chaotic. It is hard for us to keep from desiring personal pleasure and focusing too much on our bodies. But we don't want our souls to be on the path to radical ruin! We will make a relationship with You our destination. Renovate our hearts and change our paths.*

CHAPTER 9

SELF-DENIAL: THE PATH TO RADICAL GOODNESS, PART 1

> *Don't you realize that this is not the way to live? Unjust people*
> *who don't care about God will not be joining in his kingdom.*
> *Those who use and abuse each other, use and abuse sex, use and*
> *abuse the earth and everything in it, don't qualify as citizens in*
> *God's kingdom. A number of you know from experience what I'm*
> *talking about, for not so long ago you were on that list. Since*
> *then, you've been cleaned up and given a fresh start by Jesus, our*
> *Master, our Messiah, and by our God present in us, the Spirit.*
> *(1 Corinthians 6:9-11)*

One of the amazing things about the human being is its capacity for restoration—a restoration that is somehow more magnificent because it has been ruined. This is a hopeful but strange thought. Students who are into the restoration of old cars might understand this in a small way. A 1969 Shelby Mustang GT 500 is an awesome car and worth a great deal of money. Let's say you come upon one of these cars that has been left to rot and bake in a farmer's field for the past twenty-five years. It looks horrible. However, if someone takes it through the steps of a full restoration, it is a sight to behold and has great value—from $75,000 to $100,000. There is something more magnificent about it because it had been ruined. The same is true of us but in a grander way.

The key to understanding the overall renovation is rooted in what we learned in the last two chapters about human ruin. John Calvin (a leading thinker of the Christian life in the 1500s) said, "The surest source of destruction to men is to obey themselves."[1] So the only haven of safety is to have no other will, no other wisdom, than to follow the Lord wherever He leads. What is this path? It is the path of self-denial.

Doesn't sound very exciting, does it? But it does beg the question, Where is God leading us? Listen to the answer: He is leading us down a very different path from what we are used to, a path that ends in radical goodness and full participation in His kingdom. And, as we walk this path, we find that He lifts our burdens and gives us rest for our souls that are so often troubled by life. WOW! The goal of this chapter is for us to discover the steps of this awesome path.

Before you decide that the path of self-denial doesn't sound nearly as exciting as self-worship, let me clear up what we mean and don't mean by self-denial. By self-denial, we are not taking about *self-rejection*. Jesus does not demean us or take away our dignity. Also, we must not think of self-denial as a painful and strenuous *act*, perhaps repeated from time to time against great internal resistance. In centuries past, some people interpreted self-denial this way and harmed their bodies in unhealthy ways. Self-denial is, rather, an overall, settled condition of life in the kingdom of God, better described as "death to self." In this and this alone lies the key to the soul's restoration. Christian spiritual formation rests on this indispensable foundation of death to self and cannot proceed unless that foundation is being firmly laid and sustained.

A PARADOX: What do *you* think Jesus means when He speaks of the necessity of losing our souls or lives to find them again in Him? Share a practical example of what this could look like in real life. If we really want our hearts to be renovated, we need to consider this new path.

---

1. We must make God the ultimate point of reference in our world. Jesus says you must lose your life if you are to truly find it. He is teaching that you must not see yourself and your survival as the ultimate good, the ultimate goal, or the point of reference in your world. In other words, you must not treat yourself as God. By "losing your life," Jesus is not talking about misplacing it so you don't know where it is. He is talking about giving your life over to the higher calling of the kingdom of God. This means that your life is not about what you want but about what God wants. Specifically, it means that when you wake up each day, your priority and passion is what God wants, not what you want.

Jesus teaches us that if we give up the project of being the ultimate point of reference in our lives and instead focus on living out God's life in and through us, then our souls (our whole lives) will be preserved and given back to us. What does that mean? It means that for the first time we will be *able* to do what we want. "Wait a minute," you may exclaim, "didn't you just say that I couldn't do what I want anymore?" Let me explain: When we get caught up in God's life, we want what He wants. And when we want what He wants, He enables us to actually do it. (You may want to stop and read this several times to make sure you catch the power of this statement; try to explain it in your own words to someone else.)

2. Loving God and loving our neighbor becomes the new central focus of our lives. What does God want from us? Jesus said it clearly: Love God and love your neighbor (see Luke 10:27). God wants us to focus our primary energy on loving Him and others. This is not only what He wants for us, but it's also the purpose for which we were created. When we engage in loving God and others, we fulfill our God-given purpose. In other words, when we love God and others, we come alive. Could this be what Jesus meant when He said if you lose your life, you will find it? If we give up the focus on ourselves (lose our lives) and turn our focus toward God and others, we will find the life we have always wanted.

Under this arrangement, giving and forgiving become central to our lives as we take on the character truly suited to the human soul.

Most of us think of *giving* as *giving up* something—losing or sacrificing. But with Jesus, *giving* and *forgiving* are just the opposite. Jesus said it best: "Give away your life; you'll find life given back, but not merely given back—given back with bonus and blessing. Giving, not getting, is the way. Generosity begets generosity" (Luke 6:38).

Loving God and others is God's purpose for us. Now listen to what the Bible says: "God causes all things to work together for good to those who love God, to those who are called according to His purpose" (Romans 8:28, NASB). We don't have to look out for our own interests because God does. We are free to focus our efforts on the service of God and others and on furthering good in the world. And we can be just as passionate about this service as we were when we were focused on ourselves.

GROUP PRAYER: *God, we choose the path to radical goodness. We want to lose our lives so we can find Your higher calling. We will love You and others instead of focusing on ourselves all the time. We want what You want.*

CHAPTER 10

SELF-DENIAL: THE PATH TO RADICAL GOODNESS, PART 2

In chapter 9, we were introduced to the first two steps on the path to radical goodness:

1. We must make God the ultimate point of reference in our world.

2. Loving God and loving our neighbor becomes the new central focus of our lives.

In this chapter, we will look at additional steps to reverse the route to ruin and move instead toward radical goodness.

3. We must consciously practice spiritual disciplines to move in the direction of radical goodness. Because we are born with ruined souls that are bent on self-worship, continuously loving God and others does not come naturally. Therefore, as we begin this journey of self-denial and radical goodness, we must concentrate on practicing certain spiritual disciplines that will help us move in this unnatural direction.

What are spiritual disciplines? They are just like the disciplines, exercises, routines, or drills that you go through to learn how to play a certain sport or musical instrument. Very few people become excellent athletes or musicians without intense training and discipline. The same is true in the spiritual life. Things like meditating on Scripture, studying Scripture, spending time in solitude, practicing simplicity and frugality, praising God and celebrating His goodness, and living a life of prayer are just some of the disciplines that help us make the move from self-worship to self-denial.

Let me give you an example from my own life. At the beginning of my day, often before getting out of bed, I stop and think of God. I mentally turn toward Him and commit my life and the events of my day to His care. Usually I do this while meditatively praying through the Lord's Prayer and possibly the Twenty-Third Psalm as well. This puts me in a good frame of mind to meet everything that happens to me during the day as sent by God, or at least permitted by Him. I greet the day resting in God's caring hand. This helps me to "do everything readily and cheerfully—no bickering, no second-guessing" (Philippians 2:14) because I have already placed God in charge. I trust Him to work out whatever happens in my life for my good. It is no longer my job to manage things that are beyond my control, such as the weather, airplanes, and other people.

The intentional use of the spiritual disciplines will be essential for your journey to self-denial and radical goodness because, over time, the disciplines make something natural out of what was originally unnatural.

THE DISCIPLINE OF SCRIPTURE READING: For the next week, put a Bible by your bedside. For seven days in a row, as soon as you wake up each morning, open to the Lord's Prayer in Matthew 6:9-13. Or try Psalm 23. As you read these passages, commit yourself before God to live out their implications—before your feet even touch the floor. During the day, look for opportunities to live God's way as shown in these Scriptures. When the week is over, share your experiences with others in your group.

---

4. Over time, radical goodness conquers all five parts of us. With time and experience of God's love and care for us, all five parts of us will progressively harmonize better with each other. We will find the power to be generous in every way with those around us—just as Jesus was. Our love for God will energize and direct our love for our neighbor. Love for God and neighbor gradually pulls the entire structure of our person into proper alignment—our heart, mind, body, soul, and relationships with others. This renovation will determine the friends we hang out with. It will direct our minds and feelings to dwell on things that are good instead of lingering on things that tempt us toward evil. Our bodies will be used to praise God and fulfill His will instead of allowing our hearts to give in to the dead-end temptations of premarital sex, drugs, alcohol, and other negative actions.

Being dead to self is the most productive and truthful way to live. That seems odd, doesn't it? How can being dead be productive? Jesus said,

> *"Unless a grain of wheat is buried in the ground, dead to the world, it is never any more than a grain of wheat. But if it is buried, it sprouts and reproduces itself many times over. In the same way, anyone who holds on to life just as it is destroys that life. But if you let it go, reckless in your love, you'll have it forever, real and eternal." (John 12:24-25)*

There will come a time in your experience as an apprentice of Jesus when it will be appropriate to speak of your being dead to self. It certainly won't happen overnight and probably won't happen until you've been walking with Christ much longer. However, the sooner you start the journey, the sooner you will reap the full benefits. How will you know you are there? Well, this is a hard thing to say for sure, and you certainly don't want to go around bragging about it. If you do, you can be certain you are not there yet. Being dead to self becomes a reality when the mere fact that you do not get what you want does not surprise or offend you and has no control over you. You'll no longer have to give your life to looking after your own interests because you'll have become confident that God is looking after you. Romans 8:28 reads, "God causes all things to work together for good to those who love God, to those who are called according to His purpose" (NASB). The apprentice of Jesus not only believes this but also lives by it.

THE DISCIPLINE OF SERVICE: *People want the front seat of the car, the back seat at church, and the center of attention.* The next ten times you get into a car with your family or even your friends, choose to give up the best seat. Take the worst seat available. And don't say a word about it. Just do it.

5. **Our focus on God and others leads us to become the kind of people for whom the kingdom of God is truly home.** People who give themselves to self-worship give themselves to radical ruin. As we learned in chapter 8, they become people for whom "away from God" is the only place they feel they belong. But those who give themselves to self-denial give themselves to radical goodness. They become people for whom God's kingdom is the only place they feel at home.

GROUP PRAYER: *God, we will practice and exercise and retrain ourselves in Your ways. With time and with Your love, radical goodness will conquer every part of our lives. As we die to ourselves, we will become suited for Your kingdom. We deny ourselves and choose the path to radical goodness.*

WRAP UP

Let's review the principles from chapters 7–10.

CHAPTER 7: SELF-WORSHIP: THE PATH TO RADICAL RUIN, PART 1

1. Heart Ruin: Our ruin begins when our hearts reject God's thoughts.
2. Mind Ruin: After we toss God out of our hearts, our minds try to convince us that we are god—the center of the universe—and that life is all about us.

CHAPTER 8: SELF-WORSHIP: THE PATH TO RADICAL RUIN, PART 2

3. Emotional Ruin: Our feelings soon follow along the path of chaos.
4. Body Ruin: When we don't worship God, we worship our bodies.
5. Soul Ruin: Our focus on ourselves leads us to become the kind of people for whom "away from God" is the only place we comfortably belong.

CHAPTER 9: SELF-DENIAL: THE PATH TO RADICAL GOODNESS, PART 1

1. We must make God the ultimate point of reference in our world.
2. Loving God and loving our neighbor becomes the new central focus of our lives.

CHAPTER 10: SELF-DENIAL: THE PATH TO RADICAL GOODNESS, PART 2

3. We must consciously practice spiritual disciplines to move in the direction of radical goodness.
4. Over time, radical goodness conquers all five parts of us.
5. Our focus on God and others leads us to become the kind of people for whom the kingdom of God is truly home.

RECONSIDER: Go back to page 50 and reread The Case of the Stolen Boyfriend. In light of what you have read in chapters 7–10, would you take a different path now in your treatment of this former friend?

GROUP PRAYER: *Lord, we will not make ourselves or our survival the center of our universe. We will love You, and we will love others. We will practice spiritual disciplines so we can learn how to move in the right direction. We will focus on You as we travel on the path to radical goodness!*

PART 4
THE VIM FACTOR:
THE POWER TO CHANGE

Nothing between us and God, our faces shining with the brightness of his face. And so we are transfigured much like the Messiah, our lives gradually becoming brighter and more beautiful as God enters our lives and we become like him. (2 Corinthians 3:18)

Let's review. We have looked at the five parts of us that need to be renovated: the heart, the mind (thoughts and feelings), the body, the social life, and the soul. We have looked at our central problem, self-worship. We have also looked at the foundation of our renovation, self-denial. Simply put, spiritual formation in Christ is the process by which we move and are moved from self-worship to self-denial.

If our self-denial progressively becomes a part of who we are, it will have a dramatic impact on the way we live life and react to life. As we have already said, we can't make this change on our own. We need the power of God in our lives to move us to change. But we have a role in this process as well. We must be willing and passionate participants in God's work to change us into the likeness of Jesus. We will learn about our part in the chapters that follow. What is it called? The VIM Factor. What is VIM? Keep reading and you'll find out. . . .

GROUP PRAYER: *Father, we don't want anything to get between Your face and ours. We want to reflect You, and we want to shine brighter each day as You renovate our hearts. We are willing to change. We want to passionately participate in Your work in us.*

CHAPTER 11

UNDERSTANDING THE POWER OF VIM

*God is strong, and he wants you strong. So take everything
the Master has set out for you, well-made weapons of the best
materials. And put them to use so you will be able to stand
up to everything the Devil throws your way. (Ephesians
6:10-11)*

Here is the $64,000 question: How do we move from a life of self-worship to a life of self-denial? That is what we will address in this chapter. Everything I want to teach you at this point can be summed up in the word *vim*. What is *vim*? *Vim* is derived from the Latin term *vis*, meaning direction, strength, force, vigor, power, energy, or virtue. When you think of the word *vim*, think of the power that Christ has made available for us to actually experience this awesome renovation of the heart.

When you think of the word *vim*, I also want you to think of the acronym VIM, which stands for the following words:

- Vision
- Intention
- Means

These three words form the general pattern one will go through to experience change—any kind of change.

Let's look at an example. Suppose you want to learn to speak Japanese. Now, that is a hard language to learn. To pull this off, you will need *vision*. You must first have a strong desire to learn this language. You must have some idea of what it would be like to speak the Japanese language (what your life would be like after you learned it), and why this would be a desirable thing for you to do. You must also have some idea of what you must accomplish to speak the language. Why is the cost in terms of time, energy, and money a bargain considering what you will get in the end?

Many people in the United States struggle with motivation when learning a foreign language because they don't see how learning this new language will make their lives better. At the same time, people in other parts of the world are learning the English language at a phenomenal rate. They clearly see the ways in which their lives might be improved by the knowledge of English. So we can see that if the vision is clear and strong, it will very likely pull everything else along with it.

However, it takes more than vision to learn Japanese. You must have the *intention* to actually learn it. Personal transformation rarely, if ever, succeeds by accident. You must make the choice from the heart (the will) to learn such a difficult language. Sitting around day after day wondering if you will ever learn Japanese won't cut it. You must *intend the vision* if it is to be realized. That is, you must initiate those factors that will turn the vision into reality.

That leads us to the final step—*means*. There are certain steps you must go through to actually learn the Japanese language. You will sign up for classes, listen to recordings, buy and read books, associate with people who speak Japanese, immerse yourself in the culture, and possibly spend some time in Japan (that would be really cool). And you will practice, practice, practice.

So you can see the connection. Compared to spiritual renovation, learning Japanese is an *easy* example of the process of transformation. And yet, through Christ, the VIM Factor makes spiritual transformation more accessible.

APPLYING THE VIM FACTOR: To make sure you understand the VIM Factor, get your small group together and apply it to the following three examples:

- Making the volleyball team
- Planning a class party
- Overcoming a smoking addiction

If we are to be spiritually formed in Christ, we must apply *vision*, *intention*, and *means*. Not just any path will do. If this VIM pattern is not put into place and held there, Christ simply will not be formed in us. If we want the things Jesus taught and did to be the natural outflow of who we really are on the inside, we will need to apply the VIM pattern to follow His way. When our vision, intention, and means don't follow His way, we are left to the battles of daily life with no more power than a nonChristian has.

GROUP PRAYER: *Dear God, we want Your strength to be our strength. We want to catch sight of the vision of what You want for us. We will intentionally choose to make that vision a reality in our lives. We will take the steps we need to take as You direct us. We understand the power of VIM.*

CHAPTER 12

THE VISION TO BE A KINGDOM PERSON

I'm not saying that I have this all together, that I have it made. But I am well on my way, reaching out for Christ, who has so wondrously reached out for me. Friends, don't get me wrong: By no means do I count myself an expert in all of this, but I've got my eye on the goal, where God is beckoning us onward — to Jesus. I'm off and running, and I'm not turning back. (Philippians 3:12-14)

Jesus taught a vision for life in the kingdom of God. Everything He said pointed to it. He even said He was sent for this purpose (see Luke 4:43). If we wish to pursue our spiritual formation — or help others with theirs — the vision of the kingdom is the place we must start. It is the place where Jesus started.

The kingdom of God is the range of God's effective will. The kingdom is the place or state of living where what God wants to be done is done. And God wants us to be part of that kingdom. Peter said it best in his second letter:

Everything that goes into a life of pleasing God has been miraculously given to us by getting to know, personally and intimately, the One who invited us to God. The best invitation we ever received! We were also given absolutely terrific promises to pass on to you — your tickets to participation in the life of God after you turned your back on a world corrupted by lust. (2 Peter 1:3-4)

Planet Earth seems to be the only place in creation where God permits His kingdom will *not* to be done exclusively. However, as apprentices of Jesus, we long for God's will to be done on earth as it is in heaven. While the rest of earth and the people in it may not desire God's will to be done, all followers of Christ, by their new nature, ultimately desire His will. When God's kingdom will is our first passion, we find ourselves participating in that kingdom living.

A STORYBOOK VISION VS. A KINGDOM VISION: If our vision is for anything other than God and His kingdom, we live divided lives. The following excerpt describes a student, Brendon, who is torn between wanting God and wanting something else for his life. After his dad lost his job in the economic crisis of the eighties, his family was forced to move from Houston to Reston, and life for Brendon went downhill from there. Read the following description and discuss with your group where you think Brendon has gone wrong. Project ahead: Where do you think Brendon's vision will take him? What sort of vision would you tell Brendon about if you were his friend?

There is a dream that surrounds everybody in Brendon's house with what could be. They are haunted, torn apart by it, and it makes Brendon crazy, furious, impulsive. He tries to act like everything rolls off his back, but it tears at his insides. His life is in limbo as long as he is dependent, and he can't shake free of his yearning for a storybook family. So he seeks freedom on the trails, in substances, in Scouts, in church. He is a study in contradictions—a struggle for depth belied by surfaces. Though his longing of only a few months ago to be Joe Highschool is becoming paved over, there are rays of hope. The family wound is at the juncture of where Brendon seeks peace from God and repose from drugs; where he tries to please his dad by continuing family traditions; and where he flies in the face of expectations by screwing up in school. He lets out his frustration in big marks that deface the spaces of the town that he wishes were not his.[1]

GROUP PRAYER: *Lord, we will reach for You just as You have reached for us. We see that the vision You have for us is a life in Your kingdom. We desire to see Your will be done on earth and especially in our lives. Keep our eyes on that goal as we focus on Your vision.*

CHAPTER 13

THE INTENTION TO BE A KINGDOM PERSON

> *Summing it all up, friends, I'd say you'll do best by filling your minds and meditating on things true, noble, reputable, authentic, compelling, gracious — the best, not the worst; the beautiful, not the ugly; things to praise, not things to curse. Put into practice what you learned from me, what you heard and saw and realized. Do that, and God, who makes everything work together, will work you into his most excellent harmonies. (Philippians 4:8-9)*

Once we have a vision for life in the kingdom, the next step is to own that life, or to get personally involved. This calls for intention. There are two things we must intend to do to live in the kingdom just as Jesus does.

1. We must intend to trust Jesus. We must first decide in our hearts that Jesus is God, the Anointed One who brings us the truth about how we can participate in His kingdom. Let's say you were sick and went to a doctor. You must first trust that the doctor is really a doctor and that he has the right wisdom to help you get better. Part of this involves checking the doctor's credibility through the word of your friends, the credentials on the wall of his office, and his track record in healing others. In the same way, the decision to trust Christ is based on the authenticity of the words of people who knew Him, Jesus' own words and statements about His relationship with the Father, and His track record in healing the sick. When we check into these things, Jesus proves entirely trustworthy.

2. We must intend to obey Jesus. We must intend to obey the precise example and teachings of Jesus. If you went to a doctor you trusted, and he gave you a prescription to help you get well, you would be foolish not to do what he says. If you believed he had the right answer, but you didn't go to him with the intention of actually taking the medications he prescribed, you would remain sick. So it is with the Christian life.

In fact, if you don't do it, you really don't believe it. Knowing the "right answers" does not mean we *believe* them. To believe them means that we set ourselves to act as if they are true and actually follow them when circumstances call for our action. Acting as if the right answers are true means that we intend to obey the teachings of Jesus. As we mentioned at the beginning of this book, *The Matrix*'s Morpheus tells his young friend, "Neo, sooner or later you're going to realize just as I did that there's a difference between knowing the path and walking the path." In a similar way, our obedience to Jesus must make this radical shift from knowledge to action. Intention is what gets us there.

Perhaps the hardest thing for sincere Christians to grasp is the level of practical unbelief in their own lives—the unacknowledged skepticism about Jesus that permeates all dimensions of their being. This unacknowledged skepticism undermines the efforts they do make toward Christlikeness. The idea that you can trust Christ for salvation and not intend to obey Him is an illusion generated by the prevalence of an unbelieving "Christian culture."

INTENTION INVOLVES DECISION

An intention is brought to actuality only by a *decision* of the will to fulfill or carry through on that intention. Let's continue the example of the doctor. You trust that your doctor is a doctor. You go to this doctor with the intent of doing what he prescribes. Therefore, if the doctor tells you to take a particular medicine three times a day for the next two weeks, to get some bed rest, and to not play any sports for at least a week, your goal is to do just that. This is your decision even before you make the visit to the doctor. You are going to do what he tells you to do because you have a vision and a passion to get well, and you trust your doctor.

When we don't follow up our intentions with concrete decisions to act on them, this usually means that we had an ulterior motive in the first place. Say you want to go to the mall, but your parents won't let you because your homework isn't done. You promise them that you will get your homework done as soon as you get back from the mall. They trust you and let you go. When you return, you decide not to do your homework. Why? Because your motivation for giving your parents false intentions was really to get permission to go to the mall, not to do your homework.

Let's take this a step further. Say a guy who doesn't really follow Christ likes a girl who does. He quickly understands that he will not get anywhere with this girl unless he plays along with the whole "Jesus" or "church" thing. So he states his intention to go to church, to read his Bible, to pray before meals at Taco Bell, and so forth. He actually follows through on these decisions until the girl tells him that she is not interested in pursuing a relationship with him as a boyfriend. Immediately, he stops going to church, reading his Bible, and so on. Why? His vision was never to be a follower of Christ in His kingdom, but rather to get the girl. That is why this whole business of renovation begins with having a real vision for the Christian life. Our decisions ultimately expose our real vision.

LIVING OUR INTENTIONS: Mahatma Gandhi, who was born in India in 1869 and raised Hindu, looked closely at Christianity as it was practiced around him in Great Britain. He remarked that if only Christians would live according to their belief in the teachings of Jesus, "we all would become Christians." We know what he meant, and he was right in that. But the dismaying truth is that the Christians *were* living according to their "belief" in the teachings of Jesus. They didn't believe them! They didn't put their full trust in Jesus, and so they didn't have the intention of actually following His teachings. Discuss in your group practical ways you can live out an intention you have right now. For example, if you intend to spend more time with a person at school who isn't like you but needs a loving friend, consider how and when you will do that.

GROUP PRAYER: *God, it is our desire to be kingdom people. We have trusted Jesus, who is the Way, the Truth, and the Life. We intend to obey His teachings. We have decided to follow through with our intention so that our vision will become reality. We will live what we believe.*

CHAPTER 14

THE MEANS TO BE A KINGDOM PERSON

> *I don't know about you, but I'm running hard for the finish line. I'm giving it everything I've got. No sloppy living for me! I'm staying alert and in top condition. I'm not going to get caught napping, telling everyone else all about it and then missing out myself. (1 Corinthians 9:26-27)*

If we have a definite *vision* of life in the kingdom of Christ and the solid *intention* to obey Him, we will naturally be led to seek out and apply the *means* to that obedience. So what are the action steps and resources that Jesus has laid out for us that will help us achieve the vision of our spiritual transformation? Because of the vision that is growing in us for His kingdom, we are eager to discover these means and absorb them into our lives with the help of Christ and His people.

Let's go back to the case study at the opening of part 3 — The Case of the Stolen Boyfriend (page 50). We know that Jesus tells us to love our enemies, to turn the other cheek, and to walk an extra mile for a person in authority over us — someone who is already forcing us to go one mile for his or her own purposes. Ideally in this situation, we would like to be generous toward this friend by helping her with the class she is failing. However, pure will — with gritted teeth — will not be enough to enable us to do this. By what *means*, then, can we become the kind of people who would do this as Jesus Himself would do it?

The answer to this question is central to our transformation, and therefore we will devote more space to it in the chapters to come. However, for right now let me just give you the big picture. To live like Christ in situations like this, we must start by discovering and identifying the habits of will, thoughts, feelings, social relations, bodily inclinations, and soul responses that *prevent* us from being generous to this kind of person. In other words, we need to think through how the five parts of our human nature prevent us from thinking, acting, and becoming like Jesus. From this enlightened view, we can take intentional steps with Christ's help to experience an internal renovation that results in a genuine Christlike response on the outside. Consider the following as a possible list of negative means that produce an unChristlike end toward the person who has offended you by stealing your boyfriend (or girlfriend) and now wants your help.

- *My Heart's Habits of Will:* Perhaps I have grown up in a family that doesn't forgive but holds grudges. I just don't feel that I can forgive this person and then help her. It feels too awkward and unnatural.

- *My Mind's Thoughts:* What this person did is wrong. If I help her, she will never learn that she can't hurt others and expect them to help her later.

- *My Mind's Feelings:* I am feeling anger and resentment toward her for what she did to me. I didn't deserve it, and she doesn't deserve my help.

- *My Social Relations:* All of my friends agree that I shouldn't help this person. They think I'm crazy for even considering it. If I do forgive her and help her, how many more friends will she steal from me in the future? I can't bear to go through this again.

- *My Bodily Inclinations:* What was done to me makes me feel rejected and ugly. I want to feel attractive again.

- *My Soul's Response:* Considering all the points above, I just can't bring myself to forgive and help the person who stole my friend from me.

So here's the picture: My "neighbor" who triumphed over me now stands before me with a problem I can remedy. But I cannot do the right thing on the spot because my inner being is filled with all the thoughts, feelings, and habits that characterize the ruined soul and its world. My only hope, if I intend to obey Jesus Christ, is to decide to become the kind of person who *would* obey. I must find the means of changing my inner being until it is substantially like Christ's, fully characterized by His thoughts, feelings, habits, and relationship with God the Father.

If I do nothing to help myself grow up in Christ, it's unrealistic to think I will be able to respond like Christ on the spot in a difficult situation. Therefore, I am called to give my life to "off-the-spot" training—that is, becoming like Christ every day so that when a situation arises, my character will be prepared to make the right decisions. Here are some things I can do: I can retrain my thinking through study of and meditation on the teachings of Scripture about God, His world, and my life. Especially helpful are the words and acts of Jesus in the Gospels. I can also help my thoughts and feelings by reflecting deeply on the misguided course and bitter outcome of the standard human way in such situations. It is fruitful to contrast this way with the way of Jesus. I can also consciously practice self-sacrificial actions in other less demanding situations. I can begin with little steps, in other words. I can become a person for whom looking out for number one is not in the conscious assumption of life.

I can meditate on the lives of well-known saints who have practiced continuously and in real-life situations Jesus' way with adversaries and those in need. I can take a close and thorough look at the bitter world of broken relationships—at how former friends come to hate one another—to see if I want to be a part of that. I can earnestly pray that God will work in my inner being to change what's there so that I will enthusiastically obey His Son. There are many other things I can do in addition to these as *means* of fulfilling the vision of life in God that I intend.

OFF-THE-SPOT TRAINING: You've read a few suggestions for how you can practice off-the-spot Christlike living. Write down and discuss more ideas you have for training yourself in this new way of life.

What we need to notice is simply that the means of spiritual formation are available. In the spiritual life, it is actually true that "where there is a will, there is a way." This is true because God is involved, and He makes His help available to those who seek to do His will.

Of course, the opposite is true as well: "Where there is no will (no firm intention based on clear vision and practical means, or VIM), there is no way." People who do not intend to be inwardly transformed will not be—no matter what means they employ. Without this kind of thoughtful effort, God will not bring us into transformed kingdom living, into "holiness."

So the problem of spiritual transformation for those of us who identify ourselves as Christians today is not that we have no effective means. The problem is the seriousness of our intentions. Often, we do not see the great value of the work of transformation—value to ourselves and to God—so we fail to carry through with it. We do not *decide* to do the things Jesus did and said.

Notice that each of the elements in VIM feeds off the others.

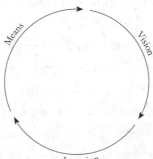

We begin with vision. Vision leads to the intention to follow Christ, which leads to actual obedience by applying the means to accomplish that vision. As we experience a little taste of what it is like to live like Christ, our vision is strengthened, and the cycle continues.

In the parts that follow, we will turn to some of the things we can do with God's assistance in *each* of the five dimensions of our lives. We will begin to experience the renovation of our hearts. As we work on the things that progressively form our inner, hidden world, we will find the radical goodness of Christ taking shape in our lives.

GROUP PRAYER: *Father, we will run to finish the race to be Your kingdom people. We will give it our all by identifying the things we need to change and by taking intentional steps to make those internal changes. We will use the means You have given us to train to top condition. We will experience Your radical goodness.*

WRAP UP

Let's review the principles from chapters 11–14, the VIM Factor:

- Vision—We must have the vision to be kingdom people.
- Intention—We must intend to be kingdom people.
- Means—We must apply the means Christ makes available to accomplish the vision we intend.

RETHINK THE VISION: On page 77, you were introduced to Brendon and his troubles. Using what you have learned about the VIM Factor, rethink the following questions:

1. Where did Brendon go wrong?
2. Where do you think Brendon's vision will take him?
3. What sort of vision would you tell Brendon about if you were his friend?

GROUP PRAYER: *God, we have the vision to be kingdom people. We intend to do all it takes to be kingdom people. We will apply the means available to us in Christ so we can be kingdom people. We will be Your kingdom people.*

PART 5
TRANSFORMING MY
MIND'S THOUGHTS

Let's say you want to go rock climbing. You ask a friend, who just happens to be an expert climber, to teach you. So your friend invites you over for coffee and tells you how to climb. He lists many steps: finding the right gear, learning to belay, tying knots, and so on. But if you've never gone rock climbing, these details will make little sense. You won't really "get it" until you actually find your location, tie the knots, and climb the rocks. And you'll definitely need your friend there with you to reiterate all the steps he listed at the kitchen table.

This example is similar to what this next part of the book is about. After reading the first four parts, you know the renovation lingo—you get the gist—but now it's time to apply it to yourself. As you read through the first half of the book, you may have thought, *This is all good to know, but how does it actually happen?* From this point on, we're going to focus attention on your life. When you finish this book, you will have your own personal renovation plan so that you'll not only know the concepts but also experience them for yourself. Considering that this isn't learning to rock climb but rather learning to change your *life*, it may sound overwhelming and maybe even a little frightening. But don't worry. The point of this book is to help you through the process each step of the way. Remember, at the beginning of this book you read that the renovation process involves taking one small step at a time. Now it is time to start taking those steps. Please hear this: Renovation is within your grasp with God's help. He won't let you fail if you truly engage with Him.

Here's what we are going to do. We will apply the VIM Factor to your parts that need renovation—your mind's thoughts and feelings, your heart, your body, your social life, and your soul. You'll learn Christ's vision for each of these five parts and be encouraged to make an intentional decision in your heart to grow. Then you'll learn some very specific means by which you can work toward the vision of a full renovation. At the end of each part in the Wrap Up, there will be a personal renovation plan for you to complete. When you finish this book, you should have a very attainable plan for experiencing the life Christ wants you to experience—a life of "inexpressible and glorious joy" (1 Peter 1:8, NIV), a life "springing up to eternal life" (John 4:14, NASB), a life beyond "your wildest dreams!" (Ephesians 3:19-20).

GROUP PRAYER: *Loving Father, help us to create our personal renovation plans. We want to see Your vision and have made an intentional decision in our hearts to grow closer to You. We need Your personalized plan for renovation so we can do what it takes to change. We want to live lives of indescribable and glorious joy.*

THE VISION TO TRANSFORM
MY MIND'S THOUGHTS

Day and night I'll stick with GOD;
I've got a good thing going and I'm not letting go.
(Psalm 16:8)

As we know, our minds are made up of both thoughts and feelings, and they're one of the five crucial parts of us that need renovation. In this chapter, we'll deal specifically with transforming our minds' thoughts, and in the next chapter, we'll tackle transformation of our minds' feelings.

The first move our rebellious hearts make away from God is prompted by our thoughts. And the first move our hearts make back toward God also comes from our thoughts. Therefore, we can and must begin to change our thoughts. It is in our minds that God first begins to move us through the words of Christ, and it is there that the Holy Spirit begins to direct our hearts to embrace these healthy and truthful thoughts.

Here is the cool thing about how God has wired us: We have the ultimate freedom and power to select what we will allow our minds to dwell on. This is impossible to do perfectly, but we have enough control to get our minds focused on Christ and to overcome the attacks from the world and Satan that seek to ruin us.

Our minds' thoughts have four aspects that work together to sway our hearts toward radical ruin or radical goodness. These aspects are ideas, images, information, and intelligence.

IDEAS

We all have ideas or ways we think about life. Some of our ideas are based in reality and some are not. The ideas are a reality check, if you will.

Many times we are not aware of how our ideas affect the way we see life or live it. It's extremely difficult for most of us to recognize which ideas are influencing or even controlling our responses to life.

Our personal idea systems have been growing from the time we were infants. They have been formed consciously and subconsciously through our experiences, the teachings of others, and observation of the behaviors of our family and community—among other influences.

WHAT IS YOUR PERSONAL IDEA SYSTEM? We all have our own perspectives, our own ideas. Sometimes our ideas are the same as our families' and friends', and sometimes they are different. Take a minute to share with a few people the ideas you have about the following subjects:

* Freedom
* Education
* Automobiles
* Death
* Family

Christian spiritual formation is inescapably a matter of recognizing in ourselves the idea system of evil we've adopted. This system sneaks in simply because we live in a fallen world. So here's what needs to happen: Our minds need to replace the idea system of evil with the idea system of Jesus. Now here's the catch: Changing our ideas is probably the most difficult and painful thing in human life. It is also very dangerous. Jesus confronted and undermined an idea system and culture, and the authorities in that culture killed Him. Because Jesus is God and He rose from the dead, He continues to ignite a worldwide idea shift that is at the core of His revolution.

THINK ABOUT THIS: Society tells us and many of us believe that to be loved and accepted by ourselves and the world, we need to be as thin and beautiful as a professional model. This belief can be very destructive to our lives. What do you think about it? (We'll come back to this idea throughout the chapter.)

IMAGES

Closely associated with our ideas are images that occupy our minds. Images are always concrete and specific, as opposed to the abstractness of ideas. Images also stir up strong feelings in us. Here are some examples of images: hairstyle (long, short, skinhead, green, orange, purple), clothes (alternative, preppy, hip-hop), flags, music, movies, and so on. Every idea system is closely linked with an image or images.

Think of September 11, 2001. When you remember the image of planes crashing into the World Trade Center, what ideas does that conjure? Perhaps it reminds you of a belief that people are innately evil or of the fact that you love New York City. Okay, now switch it. Think of some ideas you already have. Maybe you believe that war is inevitable, or perhaps you have strong American patriotism. These existing ideas influence the way you mentally process the image of the twin towers. That's an example of the way images and ideas are closely connected.

Jesus is the Master of images. And obviously, His most powerful image is the cross. The cross represents the idea of the lostness of people as well as God's sacrifice to save us. When you look at a cross, it stirs up ideas and feelings.

Ideas and images are the primary focus of Satan's efforts to defeat God's purposes for humankind. When we are subject to Satan's chosen ideas and images, he can take a nap because they're *that* influential. When we are transformed into Christlikeness, we progressively replace those destructive ideas and images with the ideas and images that filled the mind of Jesus Himself. Therefore, our minds' highest priority is to focus on our ideas of God and all the related images.

THE WORLD VS. A CHILD OF GOD: Discuss these distinctions between the way the world thinks and the way a child of God can think:

THE WORLD

Idea — To be loved and accepted by yourself and the world, you need to be thin.

Image — Magazine models and TV personalities are often very thin and popular.

CHRIST'S CHILD

Idea — As a child of God, you are loved and accepted no matter what.

Image — The cross represents the gift Christ gave you of being God's child.

INFORMATION

How are we to choose Christ's ideas and images over the prevailing view of Satan and the current culture? Two more factors exist in our thought lives that can be used by God to break the power of the toxic system of ideas and images that make us "dead to God." After God has implanted in us new life from above by the Word and Spirit, we can (and must) begin to take initiative in retaking our whole thought lives for God's kingdom. His grace will accompany us every step of the way, but we must take an active role as well. In fact, the point of this book is that we cannot be passive in our spiritual formation in Christ.

The first of the two remaining factors we'll look at is information. Simply put, without information, our ability to think has no platform on which to work. For example, if you had to write a paper for school about the current state of research on finding a cure for AIDS, but you didn't have access to the information found in the library or on the Internet, you would be stuck.

Similarly, failure to know what God is really like and what His law requires destroys the soul, ruins society, and leaves people in eternal separation from Him. The prophet Hosea said, "My people are destroyed from lack of knowledge. . . . A people without understanding will come to ruin!" (Hosea 4:6,14, NIV). Our minds can take in and comprehend information. However, if we don't have access to truth or if we have false information, we are going to find ourselves in big trouble.

Jesus made it the first task of His earthly ministry to proclaim God—to inform those around Him of the availability of God's eternal life through Himself. This is basic information for human life. It was then, and it is now.

INTELLIGENCE

The gospel of Jesus rejects any false information about God and the meaning of human life. It undermines the power of those false ideas and images that shove our lives away from God. But for the gospel to have this subversive effect on false information, we must *use* our ability to think.

What is thinking? It is the activity of searching out what *must* be true or *cannot* be true. It takes information we have in our minds and enables us to see the "larger picture" clearly and wholly. Also, our thinking can undermine false or misleading ideas and images. It reveals their falseness to those who want to know the truth. Thinking is a powerful gift of God to be used in the service of truth.

THINKING IN ACTION: Martin Luther, a professor and priest in the 1500s, was put on trial for doing some straightforward thinking about the Bible. When the religious and political courts in the city of Worms, Germany, challenged him to recant his ideas, here is what he said: "Unless I am convicted by Scripture and plain reason—I do not accept the authority of popes and councils, for they have contradicted each other—my conscience is captive to the Word of God. I cannot and will not recant anything, for to go against conscience is neither right nor safe. God help me. Amen. Here I stand, I cannot do otherwise."[9]

And so in order to recognize truth, we've got to apply the Word of God to our thinking. We can take it in, ponder its meaning, and explore its implications, especially as it relates to our own lives.

When we dwell on God as He is presented in Scripture, we'll naturally love Him more passionately, and this love will then cause us to think about Him more steadily. In this way, we enter a life of worship. When we dwell on the character of God, it's almost inevitable that we'll lapse into worship, and worship is the single most powerful force in completing and sustaining a restored person. Worship, or "astonished reverence" (as A. W. Tozer, a great pastor, mystic, and writer of the twentieth century, used to call it), is the true outcome of the renovation of the thought life.

FOLLOW MY THINKING: The progression of our thoughts can lead us away from or toward God. Consider the contrasts in the following two thought progressions:

THE WORLD'S IDEA AND IMAGE

Idea—To be loved and accepted by yourself and the world, you need to be thin.

Image—Magazine models and TV personalities are often very thin and popular.

Information—There is information available on the proper diet and exercise and the dangers of anorexia and bulimia.

Intelligence—We can use our minds to accept this information and to avoid radical ruin and move toward radical goodness. However, many people ignore this information because they want to feel loved and accepted.

CHRIST'S IDEA AND IMAGE

Idea—As a child of God, you are loved and accepted no matter what.

Image—The cross represents the gift Christ gave you of being God's child.

Information—The Bible gives us truthful information about eternal life and the identity and love that are available in a relationship with God through Jesus Christ (see Ephesians 3:14-20).

Intelligence—We can use our minds' ability to think so that we may receive and accept this information that helps us avoid radical ruin and move toward radical goodness.

GROUP PRAYER: *Lord God, renovate our hearts by transforming our minds' thoughts. Fill our thoughts with ideas of Jesus and images of His cross. Give us more of Your truth and help us to use our intelligence to study and meditate on Your Word. We want to live every day in worship of You.*

CHAPTER 16

THE MEANS TO TRANSFORM
MY MIND'S THOUGHTS

> *The tools of our trade aren't for marketing or manipulation,*
> *but they are for demolishing that entire massively corrupt*
> *culture. We use our powerful God-tools for smashing*
> *warped philosophies, tearing down barriers erected against*
> *the truth of God, fitting every loose thought and emotion*
> *and impulse into the structure of life shaped by Christ.*
> (2 Corinthians 10:4-5)

So now you've got the vision for transforming your mind's thoughts. And obviously if you're still reading, you've got some sort of intention. The intention to be transformed means that we will have God as a constant presence in our minds, crowding out every false or destructive image, all misinformation about God, and every crooked idea. To pull this off, we need to intentionally seek to use the divinely powerful weapons referred to in 2 Corinthians 10:4-5.

But without the *means* to transform our minds' thoughts, our vision and intention are useless. One of the most reliable and effective resources is discipline. There are certain tried-and-true disciplines we can use to aid in the transformation of our thought lives toward the mind of Christ. Disciplines are activities that are in our power and that enable us to do what we cannot do by direct effort. We can't transform our ideas, our images, the information we have, or even our thought processes into Christlikeness by direct effort. But we can adopt certain practices that will accomplish the job indirectly.

There are three practical disciplines that will help you transform your thought life: memorize and meditate, icons and iPods, and mentors and memoirs.

MEMORIZE AND MEDITATE

The most obvious thing you can do is memorize Scripture. This spiritual discipline can influence your mind's thoughts more than any other. When you memorize, you constantly turn verses over in your mind as you go through the events and circumstances of your life. The young warrior Joshua put it best when he said, "Don't for a minute let this Book of The Revelation be out of mind. Ponder and meditate on it day and night, making sure you practice everything written in it. Then you'll get where you're going; then you'll succeed" (Joshua 1:8).

You may say, "I'm not a good memorizer." I assure you, that's a myth. God created your mind for it, and He will help you do it. He *really* wants you to do this. As you choose to give your time and energy to the memorization of Scripture and begin to plan your life around it, the renovation of your mind *will happen*. But you must choose to do it and learn how—just like learning to program your VCR to record your favorite programs. Then you will know by experience that the mind of the Spirit is life and peace. In all the detours of life, your mind will automatically recenter on God as the needle of a compass returns to north.

START HERE: In the Wrap Up for this section, I recommend some passages of Scripture to get you started. Pick one of the verses and memorize it by the end of the day. The next time your group meets, share with each other the verses you've memorized.

ICONS AND IPODS

A second thing we can do to renovate our thought lives is to be in the presence of visual and audible images.

Icons: For thousands of years, icons have been a powerful way of imprinting entire stories and teachings effortlessly in the mind. We might arrange to have pictures or images placed tastefully on the walls in our bedroom, in our lockers at school, as book covers, and even as backgrounds for our computers and cell phones. I recall from my childhood a saying that people used to frame and hang on their walls: "Only one life. It will soon pass. Only what's done for Christ will last." This and other positive sayings constantly accented our house. They affected me powerfully because through mere habit (and a bit of photographic memory), their presence endured in my mind.

iPods: Music or anything auditory is also a powerful means to renovate our thought lives. The key is to put into our minds music and words that edify our thoughts and lift them toward an appreciation of truth and beauty. Of course, truth about human life can be sad or tragic as well as pleasant or joyful. Music does not necessarily have to carry an overtly Christian message to be meaningful. But music is best when it serves to help the follower of Christ somehow appreciate more profoundly God's presence in the world and His poignant love.

Today, we as a culture are schizophrenic about our visual and auditory consumption. We want to say it doesn't make any difference what we look at or hear. No doubt this is because we want to be "free" to listen to anything and see anything—no matter how evil or revolting. Businesses pay millions of dollars for a thirty-second spot on television. To beat the competition, they have to use more and more shock value and sexual allusions. When we see these ads repeatedly, they affect our thought lives and inevitably hinder or harm our spiritual formation in Christ. To counter these influences, we must become discerning viewers and listeners.

SUMMING IT ALL UP, friends, I'd say you'll do best by filling your minds and meditating on things true, noble, reputable, authentic, compelling, gracious—the best, not the worst; the beautiful, not the ugly; things to praise, not things to curse. Put into practice what you learned from me, what you heard and saw and realized. Do that, and God, who makes everything work together, will work you into his most excellent harmonies. (Philippians 4:8-9)

MENTORS AND MEMOIRS

The final suggestion is for you to spend time with others who have experienced the two previous suggestions with some level of success. Spiritual formation cannot be a private thing because it is a matter of whole-life transformation. You need to seek out others in your community who are pursuing the renovation of the heart.

Mentors: These are people in your life whom you can contact on a regular basis. They might be members of your own family or people in a nearby congregation of Christians. We must pray that God will lead us to others who can walk with us in our journey of renovation—whoever and wherever they may be.

Don't avoid older people; by the sheer elapse of time, they have more experience with this whole thing. We need to understand those who have learned how to seek the mind's transformation and study carefully how they've done it. However, we do not necessarily have to follow their way exactly.

Memoirs: These are books written by or about people who have experienced something significant in their lives that others can benefit from. For example, nearly every president of the United States writes a memoir after leaving office. He shares his experiences, insights, and lessons learned for all to read.

Memoirs or biographies can be a great way to motivate our minds toward Christlikeness. Working backward in time, we can read about people such as Billy Graham, Teresa of Calcutta, Dawson Trotman, E. Stanley Jones, and Frank Laubach—or even longer ago, John Wesley,

William Law, Martin Luther, Ignatius of Loyola, Francis of Assisi, and many others, famous or not so famous. How did they renovate their hearts for the Lord? We can learn from their example by making them our close companions through reading.

A word of caution: Don't look only at what these people accomplished. Look at the details of how they lived their lives and then sensibly adapt those details to your life.

There is much more we will say about the details of the means to transformation. But if we take in God through His Word and walk in the way of those who have experienced the transformation of their minds, that transformation will certainly come to us and will pervade every dimension of our lives. God will see to it!

GROUP PRAYER: *Heavenly Father, we will use the tools You have given us to renovate our hearts so that we can live a Christ-shaped life. We know that it is not our effort but the practice of spiritual disciplines that will change us. We want to memorize Your Word and meditate on it. We want to put things before our eyes and in our ears that talk to us about You. Help us to find mentors we can learn from so that we can be renovated for You.*

WRAP UP

Let's review the principles from chapters 15 and 16.

CHAPTER 15: THE VISION TO TRANSFORM MY MIND'S THOUGHTS

- Ideas—what we think about things, consciously or subconsciously
- Images—words, pictures, or songs that convey ideas
- Information—the knowledge we have, whether true or false
- Intelligence—our ability to think critically about ideas, images, and information

CHAPTER 16: THE MEANS TO TRANSFORM MY MIND'S THOUGHTS

- Memorize and Meditate—memorizing and meditating on Scripture
- Icons and iPods—constantly putting Christlike visual and audible images before us
- Mentors and Memoirs—developing relationships with Christlike people

MY PERSONAL PLAN FOR RENOVATING MY THOUGHT LIFE

I, _____, have embraced God's vision to transform my mind's thoughts and intend to accomplish this vision through the following means (put a check in each box that you intend to include as a part of your personal plan):

❏   I will memorize and meditate on the following Scriptures. (Choose as many as you are willing to commit to.)

- o   Romans 5:1-8
- o   Romans 8:1-15
- o   1 Corinthians 13

o Colossians 3:1-17

o Other: _____

❑ I will put icons (visual) and iPods (audible) before me that focus my mind's thoughts on Christlikeness.

o Icons: I will decorate my room, locker, book covers, and so on with favorite Scripture verses, sayings, and pictures that keep my mind focused on Christ and His truth. (If you have a computer or cell phone, you may want to create a screen saver using these verses or sayings.)

o iPods: I commit to filling my mind with worship music. I will purchase, borrow, or download on my iPod worship music that meets my tastes and directs my mind on the things of Christ.

❑ I will identify a mentor and read memoirs of those who can show me how to transform my mind's thoughts toward Christlikeness.

o Mentor: _____

o Memoirs (Choose as you are willing to commit to.)

BOOKS

❑ *Daws: A Man Who Trusted God* (the life of Dawson Trotman) by Betty Lee Skinnner, NavPress

❑ *Deeper Experiences of Famous Christians* by James Gilchrist Lawson, Barbour

❑ *Streams of Living Water* by Richard Foster, HarperSanFrancisco

MOVIES

❑ *Luther*, starring Joseph Fiennes; directed by Eric Till

❑ *Bonhoeffer: Agent of Grace*, starring Ulrich Tukur; directed by Eric Till

GROUP PRAYER: *Dear God, we thank You for helping us to learn and grow by creating our own personal renovation plans. We will keep our hearts, minds, eyes, and ears focused on You and Your vision for us as we practice the disciplines in our plans. We trust that if we do, You will truly renovate our hearts.*

PART 6
TRANSFORMING MY
MIND'S FEELINGS

> *Among those who belong to Christ, everything connected*
> *with getting our own way and mindlessly responding*
> *to what everyone else calls necessities is killed off for*
> *good — crucified. (Galatians 5:24)*

Feelings are both a blessing and a problem of human life. We can't live without them, and we can hardly live with them. Feelings live on the front row of our lives like unruly children clamoring for attention. Whatever particular feelings we have, they always seek to justify themselves. This is unlike our thoughts, which are able to challenge and question, "Why?" Because of this blatant nature of our feelings, they are essential to our spiritual formation. In our restoration to God, our feelings must be renovated; destructive ones must be minimized in their influence on us, and healthy, constructive ones must be heightened to a new priority in our lives.

We know, for example, that feelings move us and that we enjoy being moved. They give us a sense of being alive. Without feelings, we have no interest in life, no inclination to action. To "lose interest in life" means we have to carry on by mere exertion of will or by waiting for things to happen. This distance from our feelings is a condition to be dreaded, and it cannot be sustained for long. That is why so many people become dependent on substances and activities that give them feeling, even if the dependence harms them and those near them. Such a condition is also frequently a precursor to suicide.

So, feelings are essential to life. We must accept them and work with them. We must also be in control of them because we can be sure that harmful feelings — feelings associated with evil — will eventually be regarded by us as better than no feelings at all. On the other hand, healthy feelings are essential to a good life. If we are to be formed in Christlikeness, we must take good care of our feelings and not just let them happen.

The renovation of our feelings will be our focus in part 6. In the next chapter, you'll find vision for the transformation of your feelings. In chapter 18, you'll read about practical ideas (means) that will help you achieve this vision in your life. We will wrap up this section together by inviting you to develop a personal plan to renovate your mind's feelings.

ANGELS IN THE FLESH: To gain a better understanding of the blessing and the problem of human feelings, watch together and discuss *City of Angels* (rated PG-13), starring Nicolas Cage and Meg Ryan. One of the most common themes found in literary and artistic portrayals of angels is their desire to feel what human beings feel as a result of their fleshly bodies. In this movie, Nicolas Cage plays an angel who sees the power of human feelings and is granted permission to become human. Though the theology is pretty weak, we can learn from movies like this. The story correctly conveys the idolatry of feelings that characterizes the human outlook.

GROUP PRAYER: *Father God, we are in Christ Jesus, and so we want to renovate our minds' feelings. We don't want to set our own ways or mindlessly respond to the world's influences with careless feelings. Remove our old feelings and install new ones as we learn to take care of our feelings in a Christlike way.*

CHAPTER 17

THE VISION TO TRANSFORM MY MIND'S FEELINGS

We can't achieve the new vision of renovated feelings with a snap of our fingers. This vision requires genuine openness to radical change in ourselves, careful and creative instruction, and an abundant supply of divine grace. For most people, this vision only comes after they hit bottom and discover the total hopelessness of being who they are. Most people cannot envision who they would be without the fear, anger, lust, power plays, and woundedness they have lived with for so long. To achieve this vision, we must understand what won't and what will work.

WHAT WON'T WORK

1. Tackling our feelings head-on. One thing quickly becomes clear when we think about the power of feelings. None of us can succeed in mastering our feelings if we try to simply take them head-on and resist them by willpower in the moment of choice. To adopt this strategy is to radically misunderstand how life and the human will works.

Those who continue to be mastered by their feelings—whether anger, fear, sexual attraction, desire for food, desire to look good, reaction to being wounded, or whatever—are typically people who in their "heart of hearts" believe that their feelings must be satisfied. Instead of questioning the entire basis of their feelings, they have chosen to selectively resist certain feelings and to allow others full reign.

2. Denying our destructive feelings or dumping them on others. We all have destructive feelings (for example: arrogance, anger, lust, greed, jealousy, envy, hatred, overly zealous ambition, or the urge to belittle another person to build ourselves up), and it doesn't work to deny these feelings or try to repress them. Nor should we dump them on others by venting or acting them out. For example, if you are carrying a great deal of anger because your parents got divorced and you had to move away from your friends, you should not pretend that you don't have these feelings. And it will backfire if you blow up and express your anger toward other members of your family, new teachers, and potential new friends.

Let's be clear that it's not wise to deny feelings or repress them. That is not the answer to our problem. The proper course of action is to work toward the transformation of our destructive feelings into constructive ones that have a beneficial effect on others and on us. This will happen through the process of spiritual formation in Christ and through grace if we cooperate with God in seeking this change. I realize this process of transforming our feelings may sound impossible to you right now. In a way, it *is* one of the most difficult parts of the Christian life. But it is definitely not impossible. Please hang in there with me. Although I've compressed things here, I think this process will become clearer and more practical in the pages ahead.

WHAT WILL WORK

1. Cultivating feelings that move us away from sin instead of focusing on trying not to sin. If we are at an early stage of spiritual formation, it is a major step forward not only to sincerely desire to avoid sin but also to have a different set of feelings that lead away from sin. At this early stage, we have to cultivate two strong feelings. First, we have to develop a strong revulsion toward the wrong or destructive feelings we now have, and second, we have to at the same time develop a strong attraction to good or constructive feelings that we do not really feel at this point. This shift of our feelings proves to be absolutely necessary in order to "put off the old person" (involving the wrong feelings) and "put on the new person" (involving the good feelings). Again, hang in there with me.

Here's an example: We don't merely want to avoid attacking others verbally; we don't even want to have the feelings that lead to such an attack. And so we take steps to avoid those feelings.

Here's the power of a vision: If we develop a strong and compelling vision of ourselves as people who are free from intense vanity or longing for wealth or sexual indulgence, then we are in a good position to not to have those desires. And with our vision in place, we can then effectively seek the means (the focus of the next chapter) toward that end. The VIM pattern of change (see part 4) will work here as elsewhere.

2. Removing the underlying condition (the cause), not just the feeling (the effect). What is an *underlying condition*? It is something that causes something else to happen, even though that cause can't always be seen. For example, let's say you have a sore throat. Because it hurts, you take throat lozenges, and they ease the pain for a while. Let's say that after a week, the sore throat still has not gone away. You go to the doctor, and the doctor tells you that you have strep throat. This kind of sore throat is caused by bacteria, which won't go away very easily. To get rid of your sore throat, you must remove the bacteria by taking antibiotics. The bacteria is the underlying cause; the sore throat is the effect.

Like strep throat, if a transformation of our minds' feelings is to take place, we will need to remove the cause (the underlying condition), not just the effect (the destructive feelings). If we only deny or suppress the feelings without removing them, they will simply break out again.

The Old Testament book of Proverbs gives many examples of how underlying conditions cause destructive feelings. Jesus' brother James gives us this example: "Whenever you're trying to look better than others or get the better of others, things fall apart and everyone ends up at the others' throats" (James 3:16). Trying to look better than others or get the better of others is the underlying condition. If we don't deal with these feelings, we will continue to see our relationships fall apart. And, with everyone always at the others' throats, talk about a sore throat!

If you have a problem with feelings of anger, you can't deal only with your anger. You must identify the underlying condition that causes your outbursts and then deal with it. Only the "spiritual antibiotics" of Christ can wipe out the underlying bacteria. If you carry feelings of depression, you can't treat only the symptoms. You must treat the underlying cause, which can be many different things; otherwise, you will continue to experience depression.

3. Replacing the underlying condition; the feelings will then take care of themselves. It is not enough to wait for God to miraculously remove the underlying conditions that create destructive feelings in us. We must replace those sinful conditions with conditions that lead to a godly life and healthy feelings. We will explore God's role in a moment, but first let's deal with a dangerous strategy people commonly use to create constructive feelings.

Many people want to experience feelings like peacefulness. Therefore, they work on feeling peaceful. This is essentially trying to manage the *feelings* and disregarding or denying the *conditions* that create those feelings. When people take this flawed approach, they may avoid confronting evil to maintain the feeling of peacefulness. For example, a girl may agree to have sex with her boyfriend so he won't get angry. Or a guy may decide not to confront a friend who is using drugs because it will create negative tension in the relationship. When people try to manage the feeling of peacefulness—but not the underlying condition that produces Spirit-filled peace—they can even get to the point of using and abusing alcohol and drugs to create the feeling. This path, of course, leads to destruction and a total lack of peacefulness.

If we want to experience the feeling of peacefulness, we must possess an underlying peace deep inside. If we want to experience the feeling of love, we must possess the condition of love deep inside. This is the transformational work of our minds' feelings. When we carefully cultivate—with divine assistance—those few foundational conditions and they become prominent in our lives, the feelings fall into place.

What, then, are the essential conditions that must be present in our lives to produce healthy and constructive feelings? There are five: love, joy, peace, faith, and hope (see Galatians 5:22; 1 Corinthians 13:13). Let's understand what these virtues are and how they work to produce feelings that are healthy.

Hope and faith. Hope is the anticipation of a good that's not yet here or not yet seen. Faith is confidence grounded in reality. And for the Christian, reality is Christ. Because we have a real faith in the real person of Christ, we can see what has not yet happened or what has up to now been invisible. Therefore, we act as if the good anticipated in hope were already in hand. And because God offers the hope that He works out everything for our good (see Romans 8:28) and we believe Him in faith, we can live without fear, anxiety, and all kinds of other feelings that people who don't have hope and faith as their underlying condition experience.

Love. We love others when we promote their good for their own sake. Love is not the same as desire because we may desire something without wishing it well. We might desire a chocolate ice-cream cone, for example, but we do not wish it well; we wish to eat it. This is the difference between lust (mere desire) and love (as between a man and a woman). Desire and love are, of course, compatible when desire is ruled by love.

Here are the four movements of Christ-centered love that reside deep inside the transformed follower of Christ. These ultimately produce the healthy feelings we're hoping for. (This important teaching comes from Scripture passages such as 1 John 3–4 and John 13.)

- We are loved by God.
- We love God.

- We love others.
- Others, who also experience God's love, love us.

When love is the underlying condition of our lives, we experience the accompanying feelings of love. Love also removes much of the negative feelings we used to experience, such as fear (see 1 John 4:18) and pride. Love eliminates pride because love's will for the good of others overcomes our arrogant presumption that we should get *our* way. We are concerned for the good of others and are assured that our good is taken care of without self-will. Pride, fear, and their dreadful offspring no longer rule our lives as love becomes complete in us.

Joy. Joy is a deep sense of well-being. Its primary feeling is delight. Jesus told us that He wants His joy to be in us and for that joy to be complete (see John 15:11). When we have Christ's joy in us, we experience a sense that all is well, even in the midst of suffering and loss. When Paul was in prison, he said he had learned how to have contentment no matter what his circumstances (see Philippians 4:11). With the inner condition of joy in our lives, our feelings are not tossed to and fro by all the troubles that life can bring us. We can be freed from the feelings of fear, anxiety, and depression.

Peace. Peace is the relaxing of our hearts that results from the assurance that things will turn out all right. "I am at peace about it," we say, and this means that we are no longer striving inwardly or outwardly to achieve some outcome that's dear to us—or to avoid one that we dislike. We have released the issue and are no longer even putting "body English" or "spin" on it or inwardly gritting our teeth.

Most people carry heavy burdens of care, usually about the things that are most important in life: what will happen to their loved ones, finances, health, physical appearance, the future of society, their standing before God, and their eternal destiny. To be at peace with God and others is a great attainment and depends on much more than our own efforts. This is also true of being at peace with ourselves. To attain this peace, we can follow the advice of Paul:

> *Don't fret or worry. Instead of worrying, pray. Let petitions and praises shape your worries into prayers, letting God know your concerns. Before you know it, a sense of God's wholeness, everything coming together for good, will come and settle you down. It's wonderful what happens when Christ displaces worry at the center of your life. (Philippians 4:6-7)*

Peace with God comes only from acceptance of His gift of life in His Son (see Romans 5:1-2). We are then assured of the outcome of our lives and are no longer trying to justify ourselves before God or others. We have accepted that we are neither righteous nor even competent enough to make the crucial decisions of our lives and that we can never be so on our own. We have laid down the burden of justifying ourselves before God and are learning not to justify ourselves before men. This is the peace that grows within us.

This is a grand vision to transform our minds' feelings. In this chapter, we have covered the things that won't work to accomplish this as well as the things that will. In the next chapter, we will get down to business and present some practical ideas on how you can get this transforming process going in your own life—your own personal plan for renovating your feelings.

TEST IT OUT: Let's see if you've got the vision. Read James 4:1-6 and see if you can identify the destructive feelings, the underlying cause of those feelings, and God's replacement cause.

Where do you think all these appalling wars and quarrels come from? Do you think they just happen? Think again.

They come about because you want your own way, and fight for it deep inside yourselves. You lust for what you don't have and are willing to kill to get it. You want what isn't yours and will risk violence to get your hands on it.

You wouldn't think of just asking God for it, would you? And why not? Because you know you'd be asking for what you have no right to. You're spoiled children, each wanting your own way.

You're cheating on God. If all you want is your own way, flirting with the world every chance you get, you end up enemies of God and his way. And do you suppose God doesn't care? The proverb has it that "he's a fiercely jealous lover." And what he gives in love is far better than anything else you'll find. It's common knowledge that "God goes against the willful proud; God gives grace to the willing humble."

Answers:

- Destructive feelings—appalling wars and quarrels; violence
- Underlying cause—wanting our own way
- God's replacement cause—love and humility

GROUP PRAYER: *Father, You know how we feel and how our feelings often lead us away from You. We know that our feelings are both powerful and dangerous in our quest to follow You. We desire to experience Your vision to renovate our minds' feelings. We long to bring negative and destructive feelings under Your reign and Lordship—to eliminate them from our lives. We long to feel like Christ feels, passionate and compassionate for the right things—things that bring life. We commit ourselves to you, O Lord.*

CHAPTER 18

THE MEANS TO TRANSFORM MY MIND'S FEELINGS

Oh! May the God of green hope fill you up with joy, fill you up with peace, so that your believing lives, filled with the life-giving energy of the Holy Spirit, will brim over with hope!
(Romans 15:13)

VISION

The renovation of our hearts is going to require a transformation of our minds' feelings. For this to take place, we need to start with a sound, biblically based vision for achieving such a feat in Christ. Ultimately, the transformation of our minds' feelings is a matter of carefully cultivating love, joy, and peace in our lives. Do you see the absolute value and necessity of this vision? Without these qualities in our hearts—virtues that are placed in us by the Holy Spirit as we look to Him with longing and expectancy—we will not be able to consistently act in ways that are vibrant with the new life of God's kingdom.

INTENTION

Following the VIM pattern of part 4, we must "intend the vision" by deciding that it will dominate all we are and do. Of course, our thought lives will be focused on God. Then, through His grace we can translate our intention to dwell in love, joy, and peace into the fine texture of our daily existence. Walking with Jesus and the Father will show us the means required to bring it to pass. Do you intend in your heart to pursue the transformation of your feelings? If so, let's keep going and discover the means to achieve this in your life.

MEANS

What is our central task? We aim to increasingly possess God's love, joy, and peace as the underlying condition of our lives. When these qualities are in place in a genuine, Christlike way, our feelings will take care of themselves. Our feelings will be constructive and healthy. They will please our God and will nurture the relationships God has put into our lives.

So how shall we go about developing God's love, joy, and peace in our lives? It's basically a reconstruction project. We have to *remove* the underlying conditions that create destructive feelings and *replace* them with love, joy, and peace. Let's look at how we can do this with God's help.

1. Remove the underlying conditions that create destructive feelings in us. The first thing we must do is start to take away the underlying conditions that cause us to experience destructive and unhealthy feelings. This begins by honestly coming to terms with what our current feelings are. As we identify those destructive feelings, we can begin to probe deeper into the underlying reasons we feel this way.

We must come to terms with the deep negative feelings we have toward others who are or have been closely related to us. Wounds we have carried over the years have weighed us down and prevented our spiritual growth in love, joy, and peace. They may have seeped over into our identity. We wouldn't know who we are without them. But these negative feelings can be substantially healed if we are ready to give them up to God and receive the healing ministry of His Word and Spirit.

We must also probe the underlying conditions or motives that determine why we choose to show love to some and not to others. Paul says in Romans 12:9, "Love from the center of who you are; don't fake it." There is a great deal of "love" going on that is hypocritical and self-seeking. People can show acts of love on the outside, but they may not be properly motivated. In order for us to experience a true transformation of our feelings, we must come to a place where we can love others sincerely from the center of our lives.

Here are some elements you can select for your personal plan:

- Write a letter to the Lord identifying your current feelings or begin a journal if you don't already have one. Ask the Lord to show you clearly what your most common feelings are. Talk with others you know and trust about what they see. For example, you may carry feelings of jealousy that show up frequently in your relationships. You may express your jealousy by not speaking to others (the dreaded silent treatment) or by placing high demands on people to show loyalty to you. Write all this down, knowing that a gracious and loving God is there to catch you and carry you to a new place where jealousy doesn't rule your life.

- Name your negative feelings. Part of overcoming negative feelings is putting a label on them so that we can begin to discuss them with others and therefore acquire a better understanding of them. Here is a partial list of negative, destructive feelings to get you thinking: pride, conceit, anger, depression, indifference, materialism, envy, loneliness, gluttony, lust, a critical spirit, a judgmental spirit, a worldly attitude, worry, anxiety, unbelief, an unforgiving heart, laziness, greed, verbal abuse, physical abuse, unwholesome speech, violence. How many of these have you felt?

  Just the process of identifying and naming a destructive feeling helps to reduce its grip on us. As you work at this, don't forget to probe outwardly positive acts and feelings that are rooted in hypocrisy. For example, sometimes we manipulate people by showing kindness to them and being happy around them if we think they can do something for us.

- Identify two people who will commit to praying for you as you seek to transform your feelings. Simply put, "it takes a village" to transform our feelings. Identify two people you trust and can confide in. Share your discoveries and ask for their input. Ask them to commit to praying for you when you are together and even when you are apart. Give them regular updates so they know how to continue to pray and how to specifically thank God for answering their previous prayers concerning you.

- Journal your progress. You may be the kind of person who is very disciplined and will journal every day. That's great. You may journal only as you experience struggle or success or see these feelings acted out in others. That's okay, too. Keep in mind that at step one, you may not have uncovered the true underlying reasons you experience these feelings. As you journal, your thought process can bring to light the ideas, images, or past events on which the destructive feelings are based. Make sure you date your entries. Also, consider making all of your entries a prayer to God.

2. Replace the underlying conditions with love, joy, and peace. Receive love, joy, and peace from God and others. It is a good idea to continue using your journal to achieve this. As we discussed in the last chapter, God is love, joy, and peace, and He showers His love, joy, and peace on us. We must, however, acknowledge it and receive it. God has also placed people in our lives who have experienced this transformation of their minds' feelings and will extend Christlike love, joy, and peace to us. We need to acknowledge it, receive it, and learn from it. To begin to fill your mind with God's Word on these crucial qualities, I urge you to take the following actions.

- Meditate on these verses for the next thirty days and write in a journal the insights that come to your mind:
  - Love—Romans 8:28-39
  - Joy—John 15:9-17
  - Peace—Philippians 4:4-9

- Journal your thoughts every time God shows His love to you or to someone you know. What did God do? How did He do it? Do you have any idea why He did it? What can you learn about God and about ways of showing love to others?

- Pay particular attention every time a friend, family member, or stranger shows Christlike love to you or to others you know. Use your journal to capture the incidents and further meditate on them. What did these people do? How did they do it? Why did they do it? What can you learn about God's love and how you can show it to others? You can spot this love in a live situation or through a song, a book, or even a movie. This kind of thoughtful probing will create a positive movement toward becoming that kind of person — a person who loves. As the Holy Spirit sees you abandoning your feelings to Him and growing in your desire to be like Christ in this way, He will do His part to produce this love in the very core of your life.

MOVIE RECOMMENDATION: Consider renting *Pay It Forward* (rated PG-13), starring Haley Joel Osment, Helen Hunt, and Kevin Spacey, and watching it with your group or family. Discuss what you learn about love, joy, and peace from the actions of the main characters.

As you discipline your mind to receive love from God and others, go one step further to extend that love outward. Take what you are learning about love, joy, and peace and simply offer that to others through your attitude toward them, prayer for them, and actions on their behalf. Again, in these early stages, it is a good idea to journal about your experiences. How will you extend love, joy, and peace to other people (be specific)? Is it in attitude toward them, prayer for them, or an action on their behalf? Once you've tried this, answer these follow-up questions: How did it go? What did you learn?

There are certainly more ideas on how we can go about transforming our minds' feelings. However, these are some simple ideas that will get you moving in the right direction. Turn now to the Wrap Up for this section. Review the principles from chapters 17 and 18 and then develop your personal plan to renovate your mind's feelings.

GROUP PRAYER: *Loving Father, thank You for offering the means to achieve transformation of our minds' feelings. We intend in our hearts to pursue this change. We will remove things from our lives that cause us to have destructive feelings. We will receive Your love, joy, and peace and extend it to others. We will use the means You have given us to become new people in Christ.*

WRAP UP

Let's review the principles from chapters 17 and 18.

CHAPTER 17: THE VISION TO TRANSFORM MY MIND'S FEELINGS

What won't work:

1. Tackling our feelings head-on
2. Denying our destructive feelings or dumping them on others

What will work:

1. Cultivating feelings that move us away from sin instead of focusing on trying not to sin
2. Removing the underlying condition (the cause), not just the feeling (the effect)
3. Replacing the underlying condition; the feelings will then take care of themselves

CHAPTER 18: THE MEANS TO TRANSFORM MY MIND'S FEELINGS

1. Remove the underlying conditions that create destructive feelings in us.
2. Replace the underlying conditions with love, joy, and peace.

MY PERSONAL PLAN FOR RENOVATING MY FEELINGS

I, _____, have embraced God's vision to transform my mind's feelings and intend to accomplish this vision through the following means (*put a check in each box that you intend to include as a part of your personal plan*):

- ❑ I will seek, with God's help, to remove the underlying conditions that create destructive feelings in me through these steps:

  - o Step One: Writing a letter to the Lord identifying my current feelings

  - o Step Two: Identifying two people who will commit to praying for me as I seek to transform my feelings. These two people are:
    Name _____
    Name _____

  - o Step Three: Journaling my progress

- ❑ I will seek, with God's help, to replace the underlying conditions with love, joy, and peace through these steps:

  - o Step One: Receiving love, joy, and peace from God and others who already have them. I will accomplish this by:

    - ❑ Meditating on the following verses for thirty days and journaling the insights that come to mind
      - Love—Romans 8:28-39
      - Joy—John 15:9-17
      - Peace—Philippians 4:4-9

    - ❑ Journaling my thoughts every time God shows His love to me or someone else

    - ❑ Journaling my thoughts every time someone else shows Christlike love to others or me

  - o Step Two: Extending love, joy, and peace to others in attitude, prayer, and action and journaling my experiences as prayers to God

GROUP PRAYER: *God, we are drawing near to You so that our minds'*
feelings can truly be transformed into feelings that reflect You. We embrace the
vision that You have for us, and we intend to make the necessary changes. We
will use the means You have given us to accomplish our personal renovation
plans by seeking Your help to replace underlying conditions with love, joy,
and peace that flow from You to us and out to others. Come renovate our
feelings!

PART 7
TRANSFORMING
MY HEART

Anyone who wants to do his will can test this teaching and
know whether it's from God or whether I'm making it up.
(John 7:17)

We have come to a central topic in this book—the renovation of the heart. The words you are about to read light up a path laid out in Scripture that will lead you to the vision we discussed in the opening pages of this book. It is so exciting to think that God has made this new way of life possible through Christ.

While we have arrived at a very important step, we have learned in previous chapters that we cannot experience a transformation of our hearts without experiencing a transformation of the other four dimensions of our lives—our minds, bodies, social lives, and souls. So, we must continue to be intentional about the renovation of every aspect of our lives. But we must also remind ourselves that God is right there with us, providing us the insight we need and the power to carry out this awesome work in us.

As you read the pages that follow in chapters 19 and 20, you will see a pattern similar to the one you have already encountered in previous chapters. In chapter 19, you'll find a clear vision for the renovation of your heart. This won't be a rush job. You won't be able to microwave your heart into submission to God's will. It will involve five specific stages that will take time. How do you participate with God to move through these five stages? In chapter 20, you'll learn some specific and practical things you can do. While you will need to participate in the process, remember that it is God who ultimately performs the surgical work of spiritual formation.

The pages that follow are very exciting because they take you yet another step toward becoming the renovated person Christ has created you to be.

GROUP PRAYER: *Dear God, we open our hearts to You so we can learn how to renovate them by walking the path revealed in Your Word. We surrender our hearts to Your loving hands and ask You to give us all we need to do this transforming work. We intend to let You renovate our hearts so we can learn to really live.*

CHAPTER 19

THE VISION TO TRANSFORM MY HEART

> *Indeed, I have been crucified with Christ. My ego is no longer central. It is no longer important that I appear righteous before you or have your good opinion, and I am no longer driven to impress God. Christ lives in me. The life you see me living is not "mine," but it is lived by faith in the Son of God, who loved me and gave himself for me. I am not going to go back on that.* (Galatians 2:20-21)

God has a vision to renovate your heart. And when your heart undergoes a divine renovation, your character changes as well. Your character is that internal structure of your self that is revealed by outward patterns of behavior.

Let me give an example. Let's say you have a Christian friend named Josh who is always mean to his younger brother, Sean. Josh pushes Sean around, humiliates him in front of his friends, excludes him, and says nasty things to him. You can see how this behavior is crushing Sean's spirit, and it really bothers you. This is not something Josh has done once or twice; it is a long-term pattern of behavior. This action toward his brother is a defining part of Josh's character.

Why does Josh mistreat his brother? Maybe Josh feels insecure about himself and believes he can elevate his own status by tearing Sean down. Josh's parents may prevent him from hanging out with his friends at times by forcing him to stay home with Sean when they are out. Josh may resent Sean and therefore mistreat him almost without thought. It could be that Josh simply doesn't love his brother with the kind of love that desires to promote his good. Josh may be nice to others he feels can give something back to him, such as status in his community of friends. He may be "himself" around Sean because Sean doesn't have a choice at this point in his life to have a relationship with his older brother.

When Josh is with his friends at school and runs into his little brother, he has a choice to make. Will he positively acknowledge and include his brother, or will he ignore him or even degrade him? Josh most likely will draw on the thoughts and feelings that are currently in his mind and choose from his heart to ignore or degrade his brother. This attitude is an element of his character.

But Josh's character can change. Let's say that Sean gets hit by a car and is lying in the hospital in critical condition. Josh goes with his parents to visit his brother and sees him fighting for his life. In that moment of reflection, Josh experiences remorse and asks himself if he really wants to be the kind of person (have the character of such a person) who does hurtful things. If Josh doesn't want that, it will be necessary for him to change his thoughts and feelings toward his brother. However, just resolving "not to do it again" will be of little use. Will alone cannot carry Josh toward change. But by using his will to change his thoughts and feelings, Josh can become the kind of person who does not mistreat and abuse his brother.

Now, this is very important: Because Josh is a Christian, he has access to the Word and Spirit to help bring about this transformation of his mind and heart. Consider the following Scriptures:

> God means what he says. What he says goes. His powerful Word is sharp as a surgeon's scalpel, cutting through everything, whether doubt or defense, laying us open to listen and obey. (Hebrews 4:12)

> Every part of Scripture is God-breathed and useful one way or another—showing us truth, exposing our rebellion,

correcting our mistakes, training us to live God's way.
Through the Word we are put together and shaped up for
the tasks God has for us. (2 Timothy 3:16-17)

Don't live carelessly, unthinkingly. Make sure you
understand what the Master wants. Don't drink too much
wine. That cheapens your life. Drink the Spirit of God,
huge draughts of him. (Ephesians 5:17-18)

Josh's heart is the executive center of his life. As we discussed in part 2, the heart is the place where we choose and make decisions about what we will or will not think or do. The heart (the will or spirit) is what makes us distinct from other living things. It makes us most like God.

Josh's heart (his will) is not the same thing as his character, but his character reflects the contents of his heart. His character results from the decisions of his heart—actions that can become habitual and almost automatic in response to life around him. His character is revealed most of all in what he feels and does without thinking.

You and Josh were both created by God with a drive in your heart to do good. But that drive has been splintered by sin. So instead of asking, "What good can I bring about?" the question becomes, "How can I get my way?" I don't mean that Josh consciously thinks this through; rather, it happens as an automatic response to certain situations.

Here's a question to consider: Why doesn't God just force Josh to do the things he knows to be right? The thing is, freedom of choice is what makes us God's most precious creation. This quality of choice makes us most like Him. We are free to do what is good or what is destructive to others and ourselves. God values so highly our freedom to choose that He will preserve this uniqueness at all cost. Further, He loves us so much that instead of taking away our freedom so we'd be sure to obey Him, He paid the ultimate sacrifice. He allowed us the freedom to sin in the Garden of Eden, fully aware that it would cost Him His Son, Jesus, whom He sent to die for us—to redeem our hearts from their fallen state (see Isaiah 53:11-12).

Josh is going to have a hard time seeing the underlying reasons he mistreats his brother. He may even deny through pride that he mistreats him. Why? The prophet Jeremiah gives us the answer: "The heart is devious above all else" (Jeremiah 17:9, NRSV). Our hearts, because of their sinful nature, are full of complexity, deceit, and darkness. How then is Josh to sort this all out and see the destructive error of his ways? That's where his relationship with God comes into play. Immediately following the verse just mentioned, Jeremiah records words from the very mouth of God:

> "I the LORD test the mind
> and search the heart,
> to give to all according to their ways." (17:10, NRSV)

To God, the amazing hidden duplicity and deceitfulness of our hearts is totally transparent. Our darkness is brought into God's light. Therefore, Josh's only hope is to place his confidence entirely in God, who is willing to enter into the duplicity of his heart and bring it completely to Himself. The key for Josh is to passionately invite God to do so, "for God is greater than our hearts, and he knows everything" (1 John 3:20, NIV).

Without God, we have no hope of a renovation; that's why we need God in our hearts. Inviting God into our hearts comes in a moment of complete hopelessness in which we pray the Atheist's Prayer: "O God, if there is a God, save my soul if I have a soul." When that is the true cry of our hearts, the cry of the inmost spirits of people who have no hope other than God, God hears and responds without fail. It is as though He has a "heart monitor" installed in every person. And when the heart truly reaches out to God as God, no longer looking to itself or to others, God responds with the gift of "life from above."

HEART QUESTION: Have you ever come to that point of complete hopelessness and prayed a prayer similar to the Atheist's Prayer? I hope you have or will because it is your first step to eternal life and to a renovation of your heart.

For Josh's actions toward his brother to change permanently, he must experience a renovation of his heart. Although Josh's heart was created to do good, his nature now drives his heart to get his own way through a focus on his own desires, frustrations, or self-esteem at the expense of his younger brother. The only hope of a permanent transformation is for Josh to completely identify his will with God's will, which most definitely will spawn a caring and tender relationship with Sean. For Josh to achieve this identification of his will with God's will, there are some things he has to do. We have to do the same things to achieve this purpose.

PRAY THE ATHEIST'S PRAYER

Renovation begins by recognizing our need for God. When we cry out to Him in complete hopelessness to save us from ourselves and from complete destruction, He will hear our humble cries and make His home in us. Even if you are a follower of Christ, you may need to pray this prayer—not as an atheist but as one who is totally helpless to change without the radical work of God's grace.

SURRENDER

When we surrender our wills to God, we consent to His supremacy in all things. We recognize His supremacy intellectually, and we concede to it in practice. We may not like this humble acknowledgement of God's supremacy at first, and parts of us may still resist. But at this point in our progress toward the renovation of our hearts, even though we may not be able to do His will, we are willing to will it.

QUOTE TO PONDER: "We find the Christian life so difficult because we seek for God's blessing while we live in our own will. We should be glad to live the Christian life according to our own liking."[1]

At this stage of renovation, the center of the self, the heart, lets God be God—even if it's with little hope or enthusiasm. This might not seem like much, but many people are unable to understand the truth of Jesus because they don't trust in God's will (see John 7:17). When people are not willing to trust and obey His will, God does not open their understanding. Of course, they may reproach God for not giving them more light, even though they are unwilling to act on the light they have. Josh knows that God loves his brother and wills good toward him. He also knows that he needs to take on the same mindset as God, even though at first he may not feel like it.

ABANDONMENT

Abandonment takes our initial surrender to God's will to the next level. There is no longer any part of us that is held back from God's will. This abandonment includes all the circumstances and relationships of our lives. Of course, this complete abandonment doesn't happen all at once, and we often drift back into the need to cry out again for God's merciful help in surrendering to Him.

With this work of complete abandonment to God, Josh begins to realize that he doesn't need to tear his brother down to build himself up. God has a good plan to build Josh up and give him an awesome future of love for others.

ICON OPPORTUNITY: The Prayer of Saint Francis of Assisi[2] is a good prayer to hang in your room or inside your locker. It says,

> Lord, make me an instrument of thy peace;
> Where there is hatred, let me sow love;
> Where there is injury, pardon;
> Where there is doubt, faith;
> Where there is despair, hope;
> Where there is darkness, light;
> And where there is sadness, joy.
>
> O Divine Master,
> Grant that I may not so much seek
> To be consoled, as to console;
> To be understood, as to understand;
> To be loved, as to love;
> For it is in giving that we receive,
> It is in pardoning that we are pardoned,
> And it is in dying that we are born to eternal life.[3]

CONTENTMENT

As Josh continues to experience increased abandonment to God's will in all areas of his life, including loving his younger brother, contentment will begin to settle in his heart. He will become content with who God is, acknowledging that God ordains what He wants to and gives us the lot in life that has fallen to us. At this point in Josh's progression toward complete identification with the will of God, a spirit of gratitude and joy becomes the steady tone of his life. He is now assured that God has done and will always do well by him—no matter what.

At this stage in the renovation process, Josh is content with and even excited about his life—the good and the bad. As his confidence

in God's will for his life increa...
protect or build up his own iden...
his brother.

GREAT VERSE TO MEMORIZE: "I ...
out—plans to take care of you, not aba...
hope for." (Jeremiah 29:11)

PARTICIPATION

Once we experience some contentment, we can move forwar...
participating in God's will. We are no longer spectators but are caugh...
up in a vivid drama in which we play an essential role. We embrace
our imposed circumstances, no matter how tragic they may seem, and
we act for the good with a power beyond ourselves. We take action to
accomplish the will of God by relying on His power. Our tiny willpower
is no longer the source of our strength. It is God's power working
through us. This is the real meaning of "I no longer live, but Christ lives
in me" (Galatians 2:20, NIV). While most Christians will not fully realize
this full identification of their wills with God's will in this life, our part is
to begin the process now as best we can.

With contentment in hand, Josh is free to serve God. Josh sees
how God is working a good plan for him and that He will accomplish
it (see Philippians 1:6). He now gives his full energy to God's will.
Without question or doubt, God is calling Josh to be an instrument of
God to fulfill His good plans in the life of his younger brother, Sean.
With this kind of contentment comes a greater propensity to love others because Josh's needs are already met—or will be met—according
to God's plan for him.

The path recommended to Josh is also recommended for you. God
wants our hearts' desire to be focused on His will, not entangled an...

n wills.

...cilitate this transforming process? In the next

...ut the means (your part in the process) to real-

...novate your heart.

R: Oh God, we cry out to You for true renovation that

GROU ...ything about us. We thank You for sending Your Son, Jesus

will ch ...us, and we choose to accept Him as Your gift of eternal life

Chris ...y way to renovation of our hearts. We will look in Your Word and

and ...pirit for what we need to make this change happen. We will begin

to ...take the steps we must take to be transformed.

in God's will for his life increases, he doesn't need to strive so hard to protect or build up his own identity and selfish will at the expense of his brother.

GREAT VERSE TO MEMORIZE: "I know what I'm doing. I have it all planned out—plans to take care of you, not abandon you, plans to give you the future you hope for." (Jeremiah 29:11)

PARTICIPATION

Once we experience some contentment, we can move forward by participating in God's will. We are no longer spectators but are caught up in a vivid drama in which we play an essential role. We embrace our imposed circumstances, no matter how tragic they may seem, and we act for the good with a power beyond ourselves. We take action to accomplish the will of God by relying on His power. Our tiny willpower is no longer the source of our strength. It is God's power working through us. This is the real meaning of "I no longer live, but Christ lives in me" (Galatians 2:20, NIV). While most Christians will not fully realize this full identification of their wills with God's will in this life, our part is to begin the process now as best we can.

With contentment in hand, Josh is free to serve God. Josh sees how God is working a good plan for him and that He will accomplish it (see Philippians 1:6). He now gives his full energy to God's will. Without question or doubt, God is calling Josh to be an instrument of God to fulfill His good plans in the life of his younger brother, Sean. With this kind of contentment comes a greater propensity to love others because Josh's needs are already met—or will be met—according to God's plan for him.

The path recommended to Josh is also recommended for you. God wants our hearts' desire to be focused on His will, not entangled and enslaved by habit to our own wills.

What can you do to facilitate this transforming process? In the next chapter, you'll learn about the means (your part in the process) to realize God's vision to renovate your heart.

GROUP PRAYER: *Oh God, we cry out to You for true renovation that will change everything about us. We thank You for sending Your Son, Jesus Christ, to save us, and we choose to accept Him as Your gift of eternal life and the only way to renovation of our hearts. We will look in Your Word and to Your Spirit for what we need to make this change happen. We will begin today to take the steps we must take to be transformed.*

CHAPTER 20

THE MEANS TO TRANSFORM MY HEART

VISION

In the last chapter, we looked at God's vision to transform our hearts. While the other four dimensions of our selves need to be transformed as well (our minds, bodies, social lives, and souls), the renovation of our hearts is especially crucial because our hearts are the executive centers, the CEOs, of our lives, where all our choices are made. Achieving this vision includes praying the Atheist's Prayer (or something like it), consistently surrendering and abandoning our wills to God, and being content with and actually participating in His will.

Do you understand the vision? Do you embrace this vision? If not, I urge you to go back and reread chapter 19 to let that crucial information sink in. If you do grasp it at this point, please continue reading.

INTENTION

If you want to carry this vision through to the point where God transforms your heart and identifies your will with His, then you've got to intend this transformation in your heart—you must choose it. Because our hearts are often sluggish and are constantly bringing forth a great deal of duplicity and deceit, it may be impossible for us to choose God's ways all the time with great enthusiasm. Fortunately, all that God requires of us is to make a firm commitment to confess our neediness and surrender our wills. As you proceed in dependence on God, He will help you along the way and give you great vision for the rest.

MEANS

Now let's turn our attention to practical steps you can take to do your part in accomplishing the vision you intend.

SPIRITUAL DISCIPLINE

I want to recommend four spiritual disciplines you can practice in your life and in community with others that will facilitate transformation. When we make room for the Word and the Spirit to work in us through these disciplines, our destructive feelings—feelings we may not be conscious of that don't necessarily exhibit themselves in action—are brought to the surface and dealt with for what they are. They are our wills, not God's will. These destructive feelings are typically clothed in layer upon layer of habitual self-deception and rationalizations. Usually, they have enslaved our wills and coerced our minds to conceal or rationalize what is really going on. You'll find your mind will really "talk to you" when you begin to deny fulfillment of your desires. You will find how subtle and shameless it is.

SOLITUDE

Solitude is exactly what you think it is. It is spending time alone with God. We intentionally abstain from spending time with others to focus on God alone. How does this help us surrender, abandon our wills, and participate in contentment with God's will? The psalmist said it best: "Be still, and know that I am God" (Psalm 46:10, NIV). Our busyness keeps us from spending time with God. When we are alone, we step out of the noise of life, including the radio and television (ouch!), so that the patterns of our lives that move against God's will can be brought to the surface and addressed. As long as we keep moving at a fast pace, we will never take this closer look at our hearts.

If you study the life of Jesus, you will notice a pattern. Every time He was faced with a big decision and almost every time He finished a big event, He spent time alone with the Father (see Mark 6:31-32; 9:2; 14:32; Luke 6:12). Jesus was syncing up His life with the will of the Father. The practice of solitude helped Him—and will help us as well—to cooperate with the Father.

Although there is no right or wrong way to practice solitude, let me give you some practical advice. A good first step is to review your day in the evening while alone in the presence of God—maybe in your room, in the backyard, or on a private walk. Start with the very beginning of your day when you woke up. Recall actions and conversations, and make a note of your responses. Think about the people you ran into during the day and what their needs and issues are. Take time to confess, to feel God's forgiveness, and to pray for others. Spend a moment in silence before God, doing nothing. Breathe in. Breathe out. Sense His peace.

After you have some success at this initial level, you may want to add to the time you spend in solitude. Here is a good pattern:

- Start with five minutes each day.
- After you're habitually focusing on God for five minutes each day, try adding one straight hour each week to your time.
- Then add one whole day each month.
- Finally, to all these things, try adding one weekend each year.

As you expand your time of solitude, you may include reading and meditating on Scripture and journaling. If the weather is great, just go outside and watch a sunset or stare at the moon and stars. Believe me, solitude is an awesome spiritual experience with potentially great results.

FASTING

This is an ancient discipline that many of today's believers in Jesus know very little about. But it has great value. When we abstain from food in some significant way, we discover a lot about ourselves very quickly. Abstaining from food is a practice in which we "starve" ourselves from getting our own way. Doing this provides instruction and spiritual strength that we can then draw on as we turn other aspects of our wills over to God's will. Fasting is a tangible way to remind ourselves that our lives are not held together by food alone but by every word that proceeds from the mouth of God (see Matthew 4:4). Living out God's will as revealed in His Word is what gives us health and a solid purpose. God invented fasting as a way to help us focus on this reality. Practicing a fast is really an act of self-denial, similar to what we talked about in chapters 9 and 10. As we gain experience and success in the self-denial of food, we will find that it helps in denying other desires that seek to move us away from God's will.

Here are a few simple ways to practice fasting. Of course, the most disciplined person in fasting was Jesus, who fasted for more than an entire month. Maybe that will be God's call on your life in the future. Maybe not. But in the meantime, give the ideas below a try and see if they help you turn your focus to God and His will. During any fast, the purpose is to help you focus on Christ, so use the time you'd normally spend eating to seek God.

- Skip one meal a week.
- Eat only fruit and vegetables for one week.
- Consume only water for twenty-four hours.

Warning label: Considering the problem many of us have today with eating disorders, you should not pursue this discipline if you sense this a potential problem for you at this time in your life. If you practice this ancient discipline, you should do so with a spiritual partner who can provide mutual encouragement, focus, and accountability. If you are taking medications, you may want to check with your doctor before attempting a fast.

WORSHIP

The practice of worship simply gets the focus off of us and onto God and His will. While worship involves more than music, it certainly includes music, which is a powerful means to direct our minds and hearts toward God. Without much debate, music may be the most influential force on students today. However, worship is not just listening to music but engaging in that music through participation and focus. Worship inspires our hearts and causes us to choose actions aligned with the vision to become like Christ.

Worship is also an opportunity to reflect on God's will. We are reminded in worship that His ways are always right and always lead to joy. In worship, we reflect on God's involvement in our lives. We thank Him for what is good. We also bring to Him that which is hard or confusing in our current circumstances, knowing and trusting that He is working it all out for our good. The habitual practice of worship, without question, facilitates the renovation of our hearts.

Here are a few ways to practice the discipline of worship:

- Listen and sing along to worship music. During that time, feast on music that specifically uplifts the name of Jesus. If possible, try to take in worship music for an entire hour while you sit outdoors or lie down in your room.

- Journal prayers of worship to God. Try doing this for thirty days straight. Focus on worshipping God for who He is and what He has done for you. Start your first journal entry with the words, "God, I worship You for who You are. You are . . ." Begin your second journal entry with the words, "God, I worship You for what You have done for me. You have . . ."

- Make it a habit to attend a weekly corporate worship service in your church. Don't just show up, but actually participate with your heart, mind, feelings, body, and soul in the presence of other followers of Christ.

SERVICE

The discipline of service is the final discipline I would like to recommend that will help you facilitate the renovation of your heart. This discipline calls us to regularly use our gifts, resources, and time to serve others for their good. The key here is motive—serving others in a tangible way for their own sake. In doing so, we train ourselves away from arrogance, possessiveness, envy, and resentment. God loves this humble act of focusing on others. It helps us discipline ourselves in the surrendering and abandonment of our wills to God's. And here is the good news: Almost without exception, those who give their lives in habitual service to others, particularly to those who are disadvantaged and can't give anything in return, find great joy and contentment from that service. In this kind of action, God cleanses us from selfishness and gives us a vision for other people.

The possibilities for service are endless, but here are a few things to consider:

• Visit a retirement home or assisted living complex in your neighborhood. Develop a relationship with at least one person, and spend time with that person on a regular basis. Get to know him and learn to celebrate and pray for him.

• Serve at your local night shelter or mission.

• Volunteer at your church.

• Devote a full day (perhaps a Saturday) to being completely available to your family (or another's family) to help around the house.

GROUP PROJECT: The renovation of the heart is essentially an exercise of surrendering our wills to God's will. A longtime military symbol of surrender is the waving of a white flag. With your small group or family, make a surrender flag with a white cloth. Place this flag in a prominent place to remind you of your commitment.

Becoming one who truly wills above all to act with the kingdom of God in mind and to cultivate God's kind of goodness (see Matthew 6:33) will not happen overnight. But when we pursue a path of clear intention with spiritual disciplines and the grace that accompanies them to illumine our faults and correct us when we fail, a kingdom way of life is not as far away as many would suppose. The duplicities, entanglements, and evil intents that infect our wills can be clarified and eliminated as we keep our eyes on Jesus, who began and will finish this race we are in. Scripture tells us that Jesus "could put up with anything along the way: cross, shame, whatever. And now he's there, in the place of honor, right alongside God" (Hebrews 12:2). He calls us to join Him.

GROUP PRAYER: *Father God, our hearts are where all of our choices are made. We choose You as God of all and Savior of our souls. We choose to accept Your gift of salvation. We choose Your will for our lives, and even though it may be hard, we will take the steps required. We will begin our journeys by spending time alone with You, by fasting to build our spiritual muscles, by worshipping You, and by serving others. The path is clear, and we have decided to walk it in Your grace.*

WRAP UP

Let's review the principles from chapters 19 and 20.

CHAPTER 19: THE VISION TO TRANSFORM MY HEART

There are five ways we can identify our wills to God's will:

1. Pray the Atheist's Prayer.
2. Surrender—Surrender to God's will, even though we may not feel like it.
3. Abandonment—Abandonment is a full surrender to God's will, knowing that God is working out His good plan in and through us.
4. Contentment—Our abandonment to God's will leads to a stage of contentment with our lives that is expressed in gratitude and joy.
5. Participation—Content with God's will for our lives, we now give our lives to full participation in His will.

CHAPTER 20: THE MEANS TO TRANSFORM MY HEART

There are four spiritual disciplines we can participate in to transform our hearts:

1. Solitude—being alone with God for long periods of time
2. Fasting—learning freedom from food and other desires
3. Worship—adoration of God
4. Service—doing good for others with no thought of ourselves

MY PERSONAL PLAN FOR RENOVATING MY HEART

I, _____, have embraced God's vision to transform my heart and intend to accomplish this vision through the following means (*put a check in each box that you intend to include as a part of your personal plan*):

- ❏ I will practice the discipline of solitude.
  - o Five minutes each day to review my day before God
  - o One hour each week
  - o One day each month
  - o One weekend each year
- ❏ I will practice the discipline of fasting.
  - o Skip one meal a week and focus on prayer and God's will
  - o Eat only fruit and vegetables for one week and focus on prayer and God's will
  - o Consume only water for twenty-four hours and focus on prayer and God's will
- ❏ I will practice the discipline of worship.
  - o Listen and sing along to worship
  - o Journal prayers of worship to God
  - o Attend a weekly corporate worship service
- ❏ I will practice the discipline of service.
  - o Visit a retirement home or assisted living complex in my neighborhood
  - o Serve at my local night shelter or mission
  - o Volunteer at my church
  - o Devote a full day to being completely available to my family to help around the house

GROUP PRAYER: *Lord God, when we embrace Your vision for renovation of our hearts, our focus becomes clearer. We long to move from receiving You into our hearts to surrender, abandonment, contentment, and participation. We will practice the disciplines in our personal renovation plans as the means You've given us for transformation. And our hearts will be renovated!*

PART 8
TRANSFORMING
MY BODY

> *Or didn't you realize that your body is a sacred place, the place of the Holy Spirit? Don't you see that you can't live however you please, squandering what God paid such a high price for? The physical part of you is not some piece of property belonging to the spiritual part of you. God owns the whole works. So let people see God in and through your body.* (1 Corinthians 6:19-20)

Here's an amazing truth: Spiritual transformation is the process of forming our inner lives to take on the character of Jesus Himself. The result is that our outer lives look more like Jesus, too. Doing what He said and did increasingly becomes a part of who we are. For this to happen, our bodies must be poised to do what is good and to refrain from what is evil. The body needs to serve us as our primary ally in achieving Christlikeness.

It's important to know that our bodies are not inherently evil. However, most of us would admit that the human body is a primary, if not *the* primary, barrier to conformity to Christ. It often hinders people in doing what they know to be good and right. Because our bodies—like our minds, hearts, social lives, and souls—have been formed within the reality of human sin, they foster evil and constantly run ahead of our good intentions—but in the opposite direction.

Still, our bodies are good things. God made them for good. That is why the way of Jesus Christ is so relentlessly incarnational.* When we become followers of Christ, He sends the Holy Spirit to indwell our bodies through spiritual incarnation (see Romans 8:11). It is Christ's desire not only that we would become like Him in our thoughts, feelings, hearts, and souls but also that our bodies would be devoted to God. The Holy Spirit's indwelling gives us (if we are willing to accept it) the power to actually achieve this vision.

---

*WHAT IS *INCARNATIONAL*? The word *carne* means "flesh." When we eat chili con carne, we are eating chili with meat in it. Therefore, *incarnational* means "in flesh." The incarnation of Jesus means that when Jesus came to the earth, He took on flesh, or a body (see John 1:14).

The body should be cherished and properly cared for—not as a master, however, but as a servant of God. Most people's bodies *govern* their lives. And that is the problem. Even professing Christians, by and large, devote to their spiritual growth only a tiny fraction of the time they devote to their bodies.

But that's not true about followers of Jesus who have a vision to be transformed into His likeness. So the primary question we need to ask is this: Can our bodies truly become our allies in achieving Christlikeness? They can and they must! Chapters 21 and 22 will give you a vision and a doable path to making this a reality in your life. Of course, God will be empowering your obedience every step of the way.

GROUP PRAYER: *Dear God, we want to learn how to cherish and care for our bodies as Your servants. We want our bodies and their actions to be outward expressions of what is inside our hearts. Teach us how to let our bodies be Christlike. We give You our bodies for transformation.*

CHAPTER 21

THE VISION TO TRANSFORM MY BODY

> *Do not offer the parts of your body to sin, as instruments of*
> *wickedness, but rather offer yourselves to God, as those who*
> *have been brought from death to life; and offer the parts of*
> *your body to him as instruments of righteousness. (Romans*
> *6:13, NIV)*

God has a vision to transform our bodies. But the body is probably one of the toughest parts to give over to Christ. It is the primary obstacle to becoming like Him. Yet we can't leave the transformation of our bodies out of the journey. All five parts of us—mind, heart, body, social life, and soul—must intentionally and progressively move toward renovation. When our bodies become servants of Christ through self-denial, the results are favorable, as we saw in chapters 9 and 10. However, if we continue to make our lives, instead of Christ's life, the center of our universe, we engage in body worship that leads to radical ruin, as we learned in chapters 7 and 8.

Here is what we know about ourselves as human beings: When we don't take God seriously, we automatically leave ourselves at the center of our lives. And when we are at the center, the sensations of the flesh, the lust of the eyes, and the passion to appear important become great temptations for us (see 1 John 2:15-16).

The common temptations of the flesh involve the misuse of our tongues (gossip, lying, slander), physical abuse (rage, fighting), food (overeating, gluttony, eating disorders), discipline (laziness, sleep deprivation, too much sleep, procrastination), and sex.

Here's a scenario that should help you understand God's vision to transform your body. As you read what follows, you may feel that I'm stretching reality a bit—making the bad behavior too bad and the good behavior too good. But hang in there with me. I think you'll see the point I'm trying to make, even if my story seems to lack the "gray areas" of real life.

Let's say you have a friend named Ryan. You have been friends since you were in first grade. Now you are sophomores at the same school. Ryan's generally a nice guy but is often consumed with his image and popularity. Just this year Ryan started going out with a girl named Rachel, whom he desires to sleep with. He's been going to church and youth group meetings with you but doesn't seem to take it all that seriously. Although he hears messages about what it means to follow Christ, he hasn't made any intentional steps toward actually living that way.

THE CARNALLY FOCUSED LIFE

Ryan is what we will call "carnally focused," or intent on feeding what his flesh desires. Carnally focused people usually follow a path that ends in destructive results. This path involves the following six steps.

1. My Way: I want to establish my own kingdom. Even though Ryan has heard Christian messages and sermons and even participated in singing worship songs at youth group, he has not personally or intentionally decided in his heart to make Christ the center of his life. Therefore, by default, Ryan and what Ryan wants are at the center. He wants to be king or a god of his life. As king, he wants to be popular, powerful, and satisfied.

2. My Body, My Choice: My body becomes my primary source of gratification and the chief, if not the only, instrument for getting what I want. Our physical bodies are our primary means for getting what we want. It is only through our bodies and their energy that we can extend our kingdom. For example, a small child who sucks her thumb gains a lot of satisfaction from the direct use of her body.

In order to achieve popularity, power, and satisfaction, Ryan will need to use his body in some way. For example, he may find that playing sports brings him a great deal of satisfaction and makes him popular. That's not a bad thing in itself, but a subtle enjoyment of power can creep in. For Ryan to succeed in building his kingdom, he will want to use his body in more domineering ways. Remember, Ryan's goal is to take dominion over his body, using it toward the purposes he feels are beneficial to him. As a normal young man, Ryan is also very interested in sex and sensual things. He decides in his heart that he would like to experience sex with Rachel.

3. Your Body, My Choice: I move to expand my kingdom over others. Ryan begins to think about ways to move forward physically in his relationship with Rachel. He intends to expand his kingdom to take over hers. Ryan spends hours of time thinking of a strategy to achieve his goal. Maybe he will be extra nice to her or buy her gifts. Maybe his strategy will be to increase their physical activity step-by-step until it leads to the ultimate experience of sex. Maybe he will simply scheme to get Rachel alone and then make his move.

4. My Choice vs. Your Choice: Others who are seeking to establish a different kingdom come into conflict with my desires. When it becomes clear to Rachel what Ryan is doing, she will have a choice to make. Her choice will be based upon her own pathway. If her choice is similar to or the same as Ryan's, they will most likely engage in consensual sex. However, Rachel may have a different plan that comes into conflict with Ryan's. Let's say that Rachel has decided that she is not ready for sex or that she simply doesn't desire it as much as Ryan does at this time. So Rachel refuses to comply with Ryan's scheme.

5. War: I respond with destructive emotions. When Rachel refuses Ryan's advances, he feels rejected. Different people respond in different ways to this situation. Ryan may respond by putting a major guilt trip on Rachel. He might say things such as, "I thought you loved me" or, "If you loved me, you would be willing to show it in this way." He may respond in anger by saying things like, "If you don't do this for me, I don't see any reason for us to stay together." He may even respond with physical force by raping Rachel. This is precisely what the biblical author Jude was referring to when he wrote under the direction of the Holy Spirit, "But these people sneer at anything they can't understand, and by doing whatever they feel like doing—living by animal instinct only—they participate in their own destruction. I'm fed up with them! They've gone down Cain's road" (Jude 10-11). You may remember the story of Cain. When he didn't get his way, he killed his brother (see Genesis 4).

6. Win the Battle, Lose the War: I inject poison into my social world, and my body is betrayed. Assuming that Ryan doesn't have a change of heart, the outcome is going to be negative. Let's say Rachel stands her ground and refuses to give in to Ryan, and they break up. This turn of events undoubtedly poisons their relationship and the relationships within their friendship circle.

Let's say that Ryan and Rachel break up, but Ryan continues to pursue the same goal in his new relationships—and one day is successful. This may sound alarmist, but think about the risk Ryan is taking (to say nothing of his disobedience to God): It is possible that Ryan will end up with a sexually transmitted disease that he will carry with him for the rest of his life.

Let's say that Rachel is experiencing low self-esteem and doesn't want to feel the rejection of breaking up with Ryan and the embarrassment from her friends when they find out. So she gives in and has sex with Ryan. Ryan has won! But has he? Let's say that Rachel gets pregnant. There are a number of things that might happen. First and foremost, this is not what Ryan wanted. So he might walk away from the relationship, not wanting to deal with the complexity of being a father. He might encourage Rachel to get an abortion. Rachel likely doesn't believe in abortion, but now that she is pregnant, she may see no other way out. Of course, together with their parents they can arrive at some good choices, such as offering the baby up for adoption. However, both will live with the emotional and physical scars of their decision. Ryan wins the *battle* by getting sex, but he loses the *war* by destroying his body and his relationships.

Think about the possible consequences: Years later, Ryan may determine that his body has betrayed him. His choices were not the right choices. He will have lived long enough to conclude that a carnally focused life leads to destruction and death. If Ryan never came to trust in Christ in this life but gave himself fully to building his own kingdom, he will painfully discover that in eternity, he'll lose as well. The poison in his relationship with God will not have been resolved and, consequently, he'll have inadvertently rejected Christ. In doing so, he will have rejected an eternal place in Christ's kingdom with a resurrected body—perhaps the very life Ryan always wanted (see 1 Corinthians 15).

APPLY IT: This six-step pattern of being carnally focused doesn't apply just to sex. To get a better feel for this destructive pattern, try running through the six steps with the topics that follow. Get your parents, youth leader, or small group to join you in this exercise.

- Seeking power, popularity, and satisfaction by running for class president
- Seeking power, popularity, and satisfaction by being thin
- Seeking power, popularity, and satisfaction by trying drugs or alcohol

---

THE SPIRITUALLY FOCUSED LIFE

Christ has a different vision, a better way with a far different result. Let me illustrate by continuing to use Ryan. Once again, please bear with me. You may feel that I've made what follows seem too easy. I'm well aware that real life is harder than this and that obedience is a difficult process—not something we arrive at overnight. But, as uncomplicated as my examples may seem, I think they illustrate how Ryan's life might turn out differently as a consequence of different choices.

1. Christ's Way: I want to establish Christ's kingdom. In this scenario, Ryan makes a different choice. He chooses the way of Christ. When he comes to church or youth group, he seeks to surrender his will to God's will. Ryan takes Christ seriously.

2. Christ's Body, Christ's Choice: My body becomes my primary source to do the will of Christ. As a student, Ryan has all the temptations of others his age. He sees various kinds of media with their suggestive advertisements, and he interacts with friends who urge him to go the way of the flesh. However, Ryan understands that his life and body belong to Christ. He has embraced in his heart the teaching of Paul in 1 Corinthians 6:16-20:

> *There's more to sex than mere skin on skin. Sex is as much spiritual mystery as physical fact. As written in Scripture, "The two become one." Since we want to become spiritually one with the Master, we must not pursue the kind of sex that avoids commitment and intimacy, leaving us more lonely than ever—the kind of sex that can never "become one." There is a sense in which sexual sins are different from all others. In sexual sin we violate the sacredness of our own bodies, these bodies that were made for God-given and God-modeled love, for "becoming one" with another. Or didn't you realize that your body is a sacred place, the place of the Holy Spirit? Don't you see that you can't live however you please, squandering what God paid such a high price for? The physical part of you is not some piece of property belonging to the spiritual part of you. God owns the whole works. So let people see God in and through your body.*

Ryan has decided to embrace this biblical creed as a way of life. He has made a vow of purity before the Lord. Ryan is going to trust that God knows what He is talking about and is looking out for Ryan's good. While Ryan will date Rachel, he has made a commitment to stay sexually pure (not that it's easy, but it's a discipline he is committed to practicing).

3. Your Body, Your Choice: I will not force Christ's choice on others. Before Ryan even decided to date Rachel, he knew that her walk with God and the choices she makes were compatible with his choices. Ryan knows from Scripture that it is not wise to build a long-term relationship or partnership on a foundation that is divided in purpose (see 2 Corinthians 6:14). Christians make it a priority to pursue peace in relationships. And that peace can exist only in an environment in which people are not constantly fighting to get their own way over another's wishes.

4. Christ's Choice vs. Your Choice: I will choose Christ's choice when it conflicts with others' choices. Ryan has given Christ center stage in his life. He makes his decisions from the heart, and he plans, with God's help, to keep his commitments. As Ryan progressively experiences a transformation in all five parts of his person—mind, heart, body, social life, and soul—his commitments become easier to fulfill. Christ's choice and plan are what governs Ryan's choices. If Rachel decides to move in another direction that is opposed to the teaching of Christ, Ryan will not be able to participate. He won't be haughty, arrogant, or self-righteous about it, but he will be gently firm. His thoughts, words, and body language will be similar to that of Joshua in the Bible: "If you decide that it's a bad thing to worship GOD, then choose a god you'd rather serve—and do it today. . . . As for me and my family, we'll worship GOD" (Joshua 24:15). Ultimately, this firm decision may result in Ryan and Rachel breaking up.

5. Peace: I respond with constructive emotions. Because Ryan has followed this path, his goal is not to establish his own kingdom but rather Christ's kingdom in and through him. Christ teaches Ryan to love God and others as the priority of his life. Christ teaches Ryan to develop the fruit of the Spirit and to display that fruit in his relationships. Ryan's body and body language form the primary source of energy he has to be loving, joyful, peaceful, faithful, gentle, kind, good, patient, and self-controlled. These emotions and actions are constructive and create an environment of peace. Who doesn't want to live perpetually in that kind of place and relationship?

6. Win/Win: I inject health into my social world, and my body is honored. A Christ-focused life creates a win/win scenario. Rachel feels honored and respected by Ryan. Maybe they will date for six months or a year, or maybe they'll even get married. If Ryan stays on this path, he will experience a godly life, free of guilt from past mistakes created in and by the body. He will escape the lingering effects that sinful actions leave on the body. He will avoid the casualties of ruined relationships brought on by his insistence on building his own kingdom. Instead he will "take hold of the life that is truly life" (1 Timothy 6:19, NIV).

The body of an apprentice of Jesus has literally been bought back from evil by God through the death of His Son. It is therefore God's body to do with as He pleases, and He pleases that our bodies should be showplaces of His greatness (see 1 Corinthians 6:20).

Christians are the last people on earth who can say, "My body is my own, and I shall do with it what I please." The only sensible pattern for a human being who trusts Christ is to do what Paul urges in Romans 12:

> So here's what I want you to do, God helping you: Take your everyday, ordinary life — your sleeping, eating, going-to-work, and walking-around life — and place it before God as an offering. Embracing what God does for you is the best thing you can do for him. Don't become so well-adjusted to your culture that you fit into it without even thinking.

Instead, fix your attention on God. You'll be changed from the inside out. Readily recognize what he wants from you, and quickly respond to it. Unlike the culture around you, always dragging you down to its level of immaturity, God brings the best out of you, develops well-formed maturity in you. (verses 1-2)

That is God's vision for your body. Unbelievable and awesome! If that is your vision, turn to the next chapter to find out how to achieve this vision in your life.

GROUP PRAYER: *Father, we can see Your vision to transform our bodies, and we trust You to know what is best. We want to show the world through our bodies that we belong to You. We want our bodies to showcase Your greatness. So we give our lives—including our bodies—to You as an offering.*

CHAPTER 22

THE MEANS TO TRANSFORM MY BODY

But if God himself has taken up residence in your life, you can hardly be thinking more of yourself than of him. Anyone, of course, who has not welcomed this invisible but clearly present God, the Spirit of Christ, won't know what we're talking about. But for you who welcome him, in whom he dwells — even though you still experience all the limitations of sin — you yourself experience life on God's terms. (Romans 8:9-10)

VISION

The previous chapter described an exciting vision for transforming our bodies into the likeness of Christ. This doesn't mean that we will take on the physical look of Jesus. Rather, it means that our bodies will be devoted to God and His will, just as Jesus' body was when He was here on earth. This Christ-focused vision not only pleases God but also leads to personal health and happiness for us. God's plan looks out for our best. We have to trust Him and believe in His grace and goodness to move in this direction. I hope you have captured this vision. If this vision is not clear yet, I urge you to spend a little more time in the last chapter, perhaps with someone in your group.

INTENTION

We've already discussed the idea that we must not only capture Christ's vision but also intend from our hearts to pursue that vision. This is definitely true when it comes to transforming our bodies. When our hearts come to new life in God, the old "programs" we used to follow, which are contrary to our new hearts, are still active within us, mostly in our bodies (see Romans 7:12-18). Sinful passions are still at work, even though in the long run they can no longer "bear fruit for death" (Romans 7:5, NASB). That is because our identity before God has been shifted over to another life that is given to us as God's gift. While the spirit (or heart) is willing, the flesh is weak (see Matthew 26:41). We may find ourselves doing the things we hate (see Romans 7:15). But it really is no longer we who are doing them but rather the sin still functioning as a living force within our bodies (see Romans 7:23).

MEANS

Jesus said the heart (or spirit) must be willing. We must have the intent. However, the flesh is going to give us problems because it is already set in its ways. Jesus said the flesh is weak. Therefore, to strengthen our bodies to match the intent of our hearts' vision, we must engage in spiritual disciplines—with God's help.

So what are some things we can do to place our bodies fully at the disposal of the powerful, redeeming God who intends to live in them? I have four overall suggestions—two "dont's" and two "do's."

DON'T: IDOLIZE YOUR BODY

What does this mean? It means that you no longer make your body an object of ultimate concern. You have, after all, given it up to God's control. You have taken your hands off of outcomes with respect to your body, and you care for it only as it serves God's purposes in your life and the lives of others. You don't worry about what will happen to it—sickness, aging, death—for you have placed God in charge of all that. Any issues that arise in this area you freely take up with Him in prayer. You take good care of your body, but only within the framework of values clearly laid down by God and exemplified in Jesus Christ. You don't live in fear of your body and what it might "do to you."

DON'T: MISUSE YOUR BODY

This means primarily two things:

1. Do not use your body as a source of sensual gratification. When sensual gratification is accepted as a necessity, addictions of various kinds exist. These are misuses of the body. Bodily pleasure in itself is not a bad thing. But when it is exalted to a necessity and we become dependent upon it, we are slaves of our bodies and their feelings. Only misery lies ahead.

2. Do not use your body to dominate or control others.

   - Do not present your body in ways that elicit sexual thoughts, feelings, and actions from others. We should not try to be "sexy." We can be naturally attractive without that. This can be difficult, especially considering pressure from peers and the fashion industry and actual clothes on the racks of retailers that are designed to be suggestive. But Christ calls us to consider carefully our clothing decisions. We don't always have to give in to the trends. Also, the overemphasis in our society on bodybuilding for the purpose of looks (not just health) can become an obsession we should avoid. Don't intimidate others with your body. There are many aspects of this, up to and including brute force. The most common forms of intimidation are loud and domineering behavior, "power dressing," sarcasm, leering, and "knowing" looks and remarks. Having given up your body to God, do not use it or its parts in these ways.

   - Do not overwork. In our current world, this is a primary misuse of the body. It is now said that work is the new "drug of choice." Often this is associated with excessive competition and trying to beat out others in some area of life. Sometimes this is just a matter of wearing our bodies out in order to succeed—often in circumstances that we regard (perhaps rightly) as imposed upon us by others. But it is still a misuse of the body and a failure to work things out with God. God *never* gives us too much to do. Pressure may come from another source—such as our own need to excel or get ahead—but God Himself is not the author of an impossible work schedule. David long ago described God with these words:

> *It's useless to rise early and go to bed late,*
> *   and work your worried fingers to the bone.*
> *Don't you know he enjoys*
> *   giving rest to those he loves? (Psalm 127:2)*

DO: RELEASE YOUR BODY TO GOD

When Paul tells us to "offer your bodies as living sacrifices, holy and pleasing to God" (Romans 12:1, NIV), he is saying that the presentation of our bodies to God needs to be a definite decision and one that we renew regularly. As a crucial response to God, it isn't something we can drift into passively; we must give conscious attention to it.

Here is one strategy to release your body to God.

Step 1: Decide to give your body to God. Do this on the basis of understanding how important it is because Scripture requires it. Know, therefore, that it is a good and indispensable thing to do.

Step 2: Do a "ritual of sacrifice" retreat. This is an intensely personal time in which you find a quiet, private place where you can be alone with God. It may be your room or some other place where you can close the door and remain undisturbed. Here are seven things you can do on this retreat to accomplish your objective:

1. Quiet your soul and your body so they can be cleared of the fog of your daily burdens and preoccupations.
2. Meditatively pray some central Scriptures before the Lord (such as Romans 6–8 and 1 Corinthians 6:12-20).
3. Lie down on the floor, face down or face up, and explicitly and formally surrender your body to God.

4. Kneel before God and ask Him to take charge of each part of your body, to fill it with His life, and to use it for His purposes. Accentuate the positive—don't just think of not sinning with your body. This is an active consecration of your body to God's power and purpose. Remember, a sacrifice is something God *takes up* into Himself.

5. Give thanks to God, arise, and spend some time in praise. A joyful reading (chant and walk or dance) of Psalms 145–150 would be an excellent exercise. Put your body into it.

6. Share what you have done with your small group and/or family and ask them to bless it.

7. Review your ritual of sacrifice in thought and prayer from time to time over the following weeks and plan to renew the same ritual surrender year after year.

DO: PROPERLY HONOR AND CARE FOR YOUR BODY

The positive counterpart of the thoughts expressed in the "dont's" is that the body is to be properly honored and cared for. Here are some ideas to help you do this:

• Regard your body as holy because it is owned and inhabited by God. To immerse yourself in this idea, reread 1 Corinthians 6:12-20.

• Practice the Sabbath. Because our bodies are holy (separated to God), we should properly care for them: nourish, exercise, and rest them. The practical center of proper care for the body is Sabbath. Sabbath is a profound and intricate subject that we can't deal with extensively here. But no treatment of spiritual formation and the body can be complete without at least touching upon the meaning of Sabbath.

Sabbath fulfilled in human life is really a celebration of God. Sabbath is inseparable from worship, and, indeed, genuine worship is Sabbath. When we come to the place where we can joyously "do no work," it will be because God is so exalted in our minds and bodies that we can trust Him with our lives and our world and can take our hands off of them.

Here are some practical suggestions for experiencing the Sabbath:

- *Practice solitude and silence.* Simply put, we must spend time alone in complete silence. This is extremely difficult for most people when they first begin this critical spiritual discipline. However, the body *must* be weaned away from its tendencies to always take control, to achieve and produce, to attain gratification. Progress in the *opposite* direction can only be made in solitude and silence, for these disciplines "take our hands off our world" as nothing else does.

- *Get rest and enough sleep.* Rest is one primary mark of the condition of Sabbath in the body, just as unrest is a primary mark of its absence. If we really intend to submit our bodies as living sacrifices to God, our first step might be to start getting enough sleep. Sleep is a good first use of solitude and silence. It is also a good indicator of how thoroughly we trust in God.

  Of course this does not mean that we can just sleep our way to sainthood. Sometimes people sleep because they are depressed or sad, have a physical condition, or are just evading reality. Nor does this mean that really godly people — call them saints — do not work hard and are never exhausted. But when we give our bodies to God, we have resources that are not at the disposal of ordinary people who run on fumes and promises. We have to learn how to reach for these resources and place our bodies in the rest of God.

- *Exercise.* Develop a realistic exercise program that is focused on properly caring for your body and making it fit to do the will of God. Proper exercise gives us strength and even increases our mental alertness. If we don't care for our bodies in this way, they will eventually demand attention through some kind of health crisis. Work with your doctor and other specialists on the exercise program that is right for the body God has given you.

- *Diet.* Many, if not most, people today diet for the wrong reasons. They diet because of an obsession with the body and its shape. As apprentices of Jesus, this should not be the preoccupation of our lives. However, diet for the right reasons is totally appropriate and necessary. Eating properly gives us energy to do the will of God. Overeating or undereating makes us sluggish, weak, and sick. That's not exactly the way to treat God's precious property.

SPIRITUAL SNOOZING: Sometimes rest is the most important discipline we can pursue. Here are some verses to consider and discuss:

I stretch myself out. I sleep.
Then I'm up again—rested, tall and steady,
Fearless before the enemy mobs
Coming at me from all sides. (Psalm 3:5-6)

At day's end I'm ready for sound sleep,
For you, GOD, have put my life back together.
(Psalm 4:8)

God has made every provision for our bodies to fully serve Him in His purposes for putting us here on earth. There may be severe problems with our bodies, at least from the human point of view. We should not deny or disregard disabilities or chronic health struggles. But as Peter said, the real power of life lies in who we are in Christ. Our behavior flows out of our identity as His redeemed people: "What matters is not your outer appearance—the styling of your hair, the jewelry you wear, the cut of your clothes—but your inner disposition. Cultivate inner beauty, the gentle, gracious kind that God delights in" (1 Peter 3:3-4). Of course, we can't impose a legalistic ban on jewelry and so on (although sometimes we'd like to!). But these verses give us a clear indication of where genuine beauty, health, and strength for the body come from and of the incredible grace that lies in the spiritual transformation of the body.

GROUP PRAYER: *God, our bodies are Your home. We want to pursue the transformation of our bodies, even when they don't want to cooperate. We give our bodies to You for Your service. We will take good care of them and will not misuse them because we understand that they are Your holy temples. We will be obedient to You with our bodies, and we thank You in advance for the transforming work You will do in us.*

WRAP UP

Let's review the principles from chapters 21 and 22.

CHAPTER 21: THE VISION TO TRANSFORM MY BODY

	CARNALLY FOCUSED	SPIRITUALLY FOCUSED
Step 1:	My Way	Christ's Way
Step 2:	My Body, My Choice	Christ's Body, Christ's Choice
Step 3:	Your Body, My Choice	Your Body, Your Choice
Step 4:	My Choice vs. Your Choice	Christ's Choice vs. Your Choice
Step 5:	War	Peace
Step 6:	Win the Battle, Lose the War	Win/Win

CHAPTER 22: THE MEANS TO TRANSFORM MY BODY

- Don't: Idolize your body
- Don't: Misuse your body
- Do: Release your body to God
- Do: Properly honor and care for your body

MY PERSONAL PLAN FOR RENOVATING MY BODY

I, _____, have embraced
God's vision to transform my body and intend to accomplish this vision
through the following means (*put a check in each box that you intend to include
as a part of your personal plan*):

❑ Don't: I will not idolize my body.

❑ Don't: I will not misuse my body.

  o I will not use my body as a source of sensual gratification.

  o I will not use my body to dominate or control others.

o   I will not use my body to intimidate others.

o   I will not overwork my body.

❑   Do: I will release my body to God.

o   Step 1: I have made a decision to give my body to God.

o   Step 2: I will do a "ritual of sacrifice" retreat. (See chapter 22 for details.)

❑   Do: I will properly honor and care for my body.

o   I will regard my body as holy because it is owned and inhabited by God.

o   I will practice the Sabbath.

❑   I will regularly experience solitude and silence.

❑   I will rest and get enough sleep.

❑   I will regularly exercise.

❑   I will follow a healthy diet.

GROUP PRAYER: *Loving God, transform our bodies to be outward expressions of renovated hearts. Transform the vision we have of our bodies from a worldly focus to a spiritual focus as we give our bodies to You. We release our bodies to Your hands and will follow our personal renovation plans for transformation. As we are transformed, let people see You in and through our bodies.*

PART 9
TRANSFORMING
MY SOCIAL LIFE

> *The way we know we've been transferred from death to life*
> *is that we love our brothers and sisters. Anyone who doesn't*
> *love is as good as dead.* (1 John 3:14)

Can you imagine what life would be like without anyone else around—if you lived alone, not just in a house, but in the universe? Whether you're an introvert or an extrovert, that thought is really scary because we absolutely need other people. It's equally scary to think of living out our faith alone; it's scary mostly because it's impossible. How else do we demonstrate the renovation of our hearts? Now that we've learned about renovating the internal self—the heart, mind, and body—we'll turn our attention to our relationships with others to see how Christ can use our renovated hearts to spiritually transform our social lives. That's where the rubber meets the road.

As human beings, we are hardwired for connection with others. Ultimately, life isn't about "me"; it's about "us." So when we think about our lives, we've got to consider others. In fact, the apostle Paul went so far as to say that we must put others before ourselves (see Philippians 2:3). So we must pay attention to the quality of our relationships. If everything is going well in our lives except our relationships, then in reality, nothing is going very well.

So here's a big problem. Our world and our lives are filled with sin (shocking news, huh?). This sin nature coexists with our need for community, yet it seeks to destroy community. Unfortunately, it often succeeds. This problem started back in the very beginning with Adam and Eve. After they disobeyed God and sin entered their lives, Adam blamed Eve for his own sin (see Genesis 3:12). You can imagine how wounded Eve felt. Then their children followed the same path. When Cain learned that God preferred Abel's sacrifice to his, he murdered his brother (see Genesis 4:3-8). Surely Cain carried regret and guilt for the rest of his life. And think about how devastated Adam and Eve must have been. In today's society, there is more than a 50 percent chance that Adam and Eve would get a divorce. This is the fall of mankind, and it attempts to destroy our relationships.

God has a vision for our lives: to overcome the power of sin in us through Christ. In line with this, He has a vision to transform our social lives in such a way that we can enjoy the rich community He created us to experience. And His vision can actually be achieved. Of course, in this world we will always fall short of God's ideal for His eternal kingdom. Yet through the power of the Spirit within us as apprentices of Jesus, we can make significant progress in this life and thus experience a portion of the kingdom of God now.

Wouldn't it be great to belong to a group of people who experience genuine community? The next chapter is going to lay out that vision. Then, chapter 24 will give you the means to get this vision started in your life and in the lives of the people around you.

Always remember that you cannot experience this awesome renovation in your relationships without having a relationship with Christ first. If you have Christ and you choose in your heart to move in the direction of His vision, you can experience this renovation.

GROUP PRAYER: *Dear God, we want to learn how to love others so we can be truly renovated in You. Help us to see Your vision of authentic community. We will consider the quality of our relationships, and, as apprentices of Jesus, we will use the means You give us to transform our social lives. Thank You for loving us and for teaching us how to love others.*

CHAPTER 23

THE VISION TO TRANSFORM MY SOCIAL LIFE

"He will convince parents to look after their children and children to look up to their parents. If they refuse, I'll come and put the land under a curse." (Malachi 4:6)

THE CIRCLE OF SUFFICIENCY

WHAT DOES YOUR CIRCLE TELL YOU? Here's a way to think about your social life: Take out a sheet of paper and draw a big circle. Now, think of the people in your life (family, friends, coworkers, pastors and youth leaders, teachers, neighbors, and so on). Draw a figure in the circle for each person and identify each with a name. If you have time or are the "artsy" type, you may want to get a poster and use real pictures.

What does your circle look like? Are there lots of figures? Are there only a few? Consider what your circle says about you and your social life. If your circle is filled to the edges with figures, with how many of those people do you have a meaningful relationship? If there are very few figures, why is that? Are you simply more of an "inner circle" kind of person, or are you withdrawing from others? Knowing this is crucial as you begin renovating your social life.

Whatever your circle looks like, the figures represent the people God has placed in your circle of life. He desires that circle to be sufficient for you and everyone in it. What does that mean? Webster defines *sufficient* as "enough to meet the needs of a situation."[1] God wants us all to belong to a circle—a family that works together for everyone's good. "Reciprocal rootedness" is a fancy way of saying it. It means that we are rooted in each other's lives, tied together for our mutual benefit. "I am for you; you are for me" is the way God intends things to be in this circle.

In parts of Africa, a word used to refer to the community is *Unbutu*. This word can be translated, "We are; therefore, I am." What does this mean? It means that we cannot fully understand ourselves apart from others in the community. It means that our identities as individuals are formed and understood by the community or circle. Our souls, then, as we stated in chapter 5, are the sum total of the other four dimensions—heart, mind, body, and social life—including the people who are in our circles. These people are part of who we are.

Now read carefully. Ultimately, every human circle is doomed to break down if it is not engaged in the only genuinely self-sufficient circle there is: the Father, Son, and Holy Spirit. All broken circles must ultimately find their healing there.

Only when rooted in the divine Trinitarian circle (Father, Son, and Holy Spirit) can broken individuals recover from the wounds received in their circles of origin—childhood and young adulthood—and find wholeness on their long journey from the womb to the eternal city of God.

It's no surprise that there are a lot of broken circles in our society today. Maybe you are in one. If so, you are certainly not alone in your brokenness and loneliness. Most people know a great deal about being rejected or left out or not being welcome or accepted. This kind of rejection often begins when a child is born into a dysfunctional family. But we can also experience it as we get older. Unfaithfulness, divorce, failure to make it in a career, disloyalty of children—so many sins and human circumstances break up our circles of sufficiency. They leave us disconnected from others. This lack of nourishment from deep connections with others results in spiritual starvation and loss of wholeness in every part of us.

TWO ACTIONS THAT WRECK OUR RELATIONSHIPS: ATTACK AND WITHDRAWAL

When we talk about spiritual formation of our social lives, unfortunately we have to start from our woundedness. It is hard to imagine anyone in this world who has not been deeply injured in his or her relationships with others. The poison of sin in our social world is fairly easy to describe but extremely hard to deal with.

Two kinds of action can wreck our relationships: attack or withdrawal. We can verbally or physically hurt another person through an assault of some kind. Or we can withdraw from, ignore, or act as though we just don't care about another person. Either action—attack or withdrawal—can be extremely damaging. Yet these two things are so much a part of ordinary human existence that most people think they are just "reality" and never imagine that we could live without them.

If spiritual formation in Christ is to succeed, however, the power of these two forms of evil in our own lives must be broken. So far as it is possible, these actions must be eliminated from our circles. It is likely that we will not see the total elimination of them in our world until Christ comes and establishes the full expression of His eternal kingdom. But we can lessen them within our own selves. We *can* live without them. Let's look at each of them individually.

Attack. We attack or assault others when we act against what is good for them, even with their consent. The most well-known forms of assault are dealt with in the last six of the Ten Commandments found in Exodus 20:12-17:

- Commandment 5: Honor your father and mother
- Commandment 6: No murder
- Commandment 7: No adultery
- Commandment 8: No stealing

- Commandment 9:   No lies about your neighbor
- Commandment 10:   No lusting after your neighbor's spouse or possessions

Most of these commandments are self-explanatory. Number 5, however, is more complex than it first appears. Often we find out later in life how decisive our relationship with our parents is. It's wise to examine this one carefully at every age to see how subtle attack and withdrawal can be in a family. Also, number 10—lusting or covetousness—leads to many kinds of problems. This is one to watch as well, for lust is almost always a temptation.

Withdrawal. We withdraw from others when we regard their well-being and goodness as matters of indifference to us—or perhaps go so far as to despise them. We don't care. We attack and withdraw from the people who are closest to us more than from anyone else. These are the bonds that are the most immediate, intense, and potentially long-term, and so they are the most subject to attention or abuse. God gives us our families, friends, and acquaintances at school as a fertile training ground for developing our social lives.

RECLAIMING COMMUNITY THROUGH TRINITARIAN LOVE

How can we reclaim our circles of sufficiency? How can we repair the brokenness that comes from attack and withdrawal? As you might suspect, it involves our relationships with God. Growing in our relationships with God affects who we are. We experience a transformation in our hearts, thoughts, feelings, and bodies. This transformation then modifies our relationships to everyone around us. Our relationships to others also modify us and deeply affect our relationships with God. Hence, our personal transformation and our relationship transformation are interdependent. (You may need to read this section again to get it—it is really important!)

As we grow in our relationships with God, we come face-to-face with His love. God is an intimate society of love, a three-person community where there is not only love but also *shared* love for others—namely you. Within the Trinity there is, I believe, not even a thought of first, second, and third. There is no subordination within the Trinity because God simply doesn't think in those terms.

Here is something to chew on: The very nature of personality is inherently communal. The purest example is the Trinity—Father, Son, and Holy Spirit. Some theologians define the Trinity as "three persons and yet one essence." Genesis 1:26-27 tells us that we were created in the image of God. That must mean that we are communal in essence. That is, we are distinct and separate people, and yet others in our lives make up a part of who we are—our social dimensions. Our essence, or souls, cannot be adequately described and understood apart from the people in our lives.

"The individual, when isolated, is not self-suffing, and therefore he is like a part in relation to the whole. But whoever is unable to live in society, or who has no need of it because he is sufficient for himself, must be either a beast or a god." —*Aristotle*

I think this is what Jesus was telling us in John 17:20-23:

> *"I'm praying not only for them*
> *But also for those who will believe in me*
> *Because of them and their witness about me.*
> *The goal is for all of them to become one heart and mind—*
> *Just as you, Father, are in me and I in you,*
> *So they might be one heart and mind with us.*
> *Then the world might believe that you, in fact, sent me.*
> *The same glory you gave me, I gave them,*
> *So they'll be as unified and together as we are—*

I in them and you in me.
Then they'll be mature in this oneness,
And give the godless world evidence
That you've sent me and loved them
In the same way you've loved me."

That's pretty profound stuff. The love and unity that is experienced in the Godhead is now in us, and we are in God. As we grow in our connection with God, His love is shed abroad in our hearts so that we can release it to those who are in our circles or social dimensions.

Here is Jesus' grand vision: We can reclaim our community, an inseparable part of us, through the love of God that is in us. John later put it this way: "Everyone who confesses that Jesus is God's Son participates continuously in an intimate relationship with God. We know it so well, we've embraced it heart and soul, this love that comes from God. God is love. When we take up permanent residence in a life of love, we live in God and God lives in us" (1 John 4:15-16). The only way we can restore the quality of our human community is to restore our relationships with the divine community—Father, Son, and Holy Spirit.

THE PLACE TO BEGIN: THE FAMILY

Where do we begin this vision of restoring our human community? Without question, we need to begin with our own families. If we begin there, we will effect the most amount of change in our society over time.

There is so much domestic violence in our culture. In addition to violent attacks on each other both verbally and physically, there are acts of withdrawal—contempt, coldness, and noninvolvement. This is true in Christian and nonChristian homes alike. We understand, then, that we must do more than just take on the label of "Christian." We must actually strive to be Christ's apprentices.

Let's begin with marriage. We all know that the divorce rate in America today is very high. But the problem is not divorce, though divorce generates a set of problems all its own. The problem is that people don't know how to be married.

To be married is to give oneself to another person in the most intimate and exclusive of human relationships. It involves supporting him or her for good in every way possible—physically, emotionally, and spiritually. This mutual submission to each other in awe of the Lord, which is the vision of marriage in Christ, eliminates both assault and withdrawal from this most basic of human relationships. It is in a loving family such as this that children are able to participate in a whole and healthy human community under God.

In our day, individual desire has come to be the standard and rule of everything. How are we to serve one another in intimate relationships if individual desire is the standard we live by? What if the things we desire can be acquired from many competing providers, for example from other people or activities outside the marriage?

The ways in which man and wife or parents and children "naturally" fulfill one another as a family are increasingly being taken over by pervasive product marketing. We have become a nation of consumers, and our expectations keep getting ratcheted up by advertising. This is true all the way from food, clothing, entertainment, attractiveness, romance, and sexual gratification, to surrogate "motherhood" and "fatherhood." Just watch television commercials to see the fierce competition to sell products and services to individual members of the family. Tapping the desires of the consumer is accepted as the principle that governs everything.

What, then, does devotion to another mean when one or both parties are constantly shopping for a "better deal" or constantly appraising one another in the light of convenient alternatives? Withdrawal, rejection, and assault will naturally become a constant factor in the most intimate of human relations. This is what Satan has always used to defeat God's plans for human community on earth. If he can destroy the wholeness in family community, he can stall spiritual formation in the lives of individuals because we need the whole community to grow.

If Satan contributes to the destruction of a family, a person's spirituality, especially at a young age, can become very malformed (which is exactly what Satan wants). You may have experienced something like this in your own family, or you may have friends at school whose families are a total mess. You or they may act as if it's no big deal, but underneath the skin of pretending, your spirit can be crushed. When we're young, our souls, bodies, and minds can't help but absorb the way our parents and other adults in our lives assault and withdraw from each other.

Unfortunately, when it gets really bad, it seems that the only hope for survival is to become hardened. This amounts to a constant posture of withdrawal, even from oneself. Even worse, hardened and lonely souls become susceptible to addiction, aggression, isolation, self-destructive behavior, and for some people, even extreme violence.

This is why it is important to start with the family. Marching onward in life, young people grow up, and as they do, they take their hardened souls with them into their professions, citizenship, and leadership. From them proceeds the next generation of wounded souls. Our families are often the determining factor of how we will live in relationship to others, inside and outside our families.

Therefore, we've got to look at the marriage relationship—how men and women exist together in our world. If that relationship is damaged in any of its many dimensions, all who are influenced by it will also be damaged. And they will be further damaged by a surrounding world of similarly damaged people, who are trying to manage the way they relate with others on the assumption that attack and withdrawal are just "facts of life." Consequently, spiritual formation and all our efforts as

Christians to minister to people must focus on this most central human relationship.

There is no human answer to human problems. Followers of Jesus must return to His transcendent power. We can trust Christ to drain our attack and withdrawal tendencies. After all, as we know, it takes three to get married (the third, of course, is God). From a Christ-centered starting point, God's power can break the hold that attack and withdrawal have over the social dimension of the human self.

A WORD TO THOSE WHO COME FROM BROKEN OR DYSFUNCTIONAL HOMES: Sadly, you may not be able to do anything to turn your family around—at least not overnight. However, you can decide that you are going to start a new trend in your family. Beginning with you, there is going to be a commitment to Jesus Christ. Generations to come will look back to your faith in God and commitment to be a fully devoted follower of Jesus as the beginning of their faith heritage. Many people are counting on your renovation of the heart!

GROUP PRAYER: *Heavenly Father, thank You for the many people You have placed in our circles of life. We want our circles to be sufficient, and we need You to heal the broken parts of unfaithfulness, failure, disloyalty, and selfishness. Teach us how to eliminate our natural responses of attack and withdrawal and transform us by Your sweet society of love. We want to reclaim our community through Your love that is inside of us. We commit our lives to the people yet to come by asking You to renovate our hearts with love!*

CHAPTER 24

THE MEANS TO TRANSFORM MY SOCIAL LIFE

> *Love from the center of who you are; don't fake it. Run for dear life from evil; hold on for dear life to good. Be good friends who love deeply; practice playing second fiddle.* (Romans 12:9-10)

VISION

God's vision for transforming our social lives is so exciting. We all desire to belong to a family and community where we can experience reciprocal love. God has not only desired this for us, but He's actually provided the way to experience it.

God's vision is for His followers to be in a "circle of sufficiency," that is, to belong to a community that is rooted in Him.

We have access to this kind of community when we center our lives in the Trinitarian community—the Father, Son, and Holy Spirit. This community works perfectly. When God is ruling in our hearts, we experience His love for us. With this love growing in us, we can offer it to those in our circles. And as they walk with God, they will hopefully return the same kind of love to us. Of course, it doesn't always happen this way. You'll encounter—just as Jesus did here on earth—many times when love will not be returned. But that doesn't matter. Our job is to receive love from Christ and to give it away to others. This is God's vision, and it is possible only through an active relationship with the Trinity. While we will likely not experience this in full force until Christ returns to establish His eternal kingdom, we can experience it in such a way that it is sufficient—"enough to meet the needs of the situation."

INTENTION

Is this something you are interested in possessing? Are you passionate enough about living in a healthy social community to do what Jesus is going to tell you to do as His student? In other words, do you have the intent to pursue God's vision for your social life?

MEANS

What will this look like in ordinary human relations? It must start with our relationships with other believers. It is with other Christians that we will have the real opportunity to experience the fullest expression of God's vision for our communities. For it to work, every Christian must purposefully move toward maturity in all five areas of their being. The most immediate application will be in their families. There are four specific means available to you to bring about the transformation of your social life.

RECEIVE YOUR NEW ID IN CHRIST

Most schools require students to have a student ID. These cards identify who you are to the school. They usually display your name, your picture, and possibly a number that the school uses to keep a file of records on you. This identification card gives you access to many of the places others are not permitted to be. It is a formal way of saying you belong to that school community. Beyond school, we have social security numbers, driver's licenses, and passports that serve the same function.

When we trusted Christ to establish us in an eternal relationship with God, we received a new ID. It grants us access to a new way of life. In the Bible, Paul writes, "Your old life is dead. Your new life, which is your real life—even though invisible to spectators—is with Christ in God. He is your life" (Colossians 3:3). In our new identity in Christ, we find that God is our sufficiency and that He restores us to be whole people. This enables us to draw out all of the poison we have received in our relationships with others. It enables us to move forward with sincere forgiveness and blessing toward them. Only in this way can we be free from the wounds of the past and from those who have attacked or forsaken us.

We need to *daily* receive and embrace the reality of this new identity. Each day we need to claim this promise: *My life in Christ is whole and blessed, no matter what has or has not been done to me and no matter how shamefully my human circles of sufficiency have been violated.*

LOSE THE MASK

The second thing we can do to participate with God in transforming our social lives is to lose the mask. What is the mask? A mask is anything that prevents us from being real. We wear masks to protect ourselves from attacks or withdrawal. We also wear masks to make ourselves look good. Sometimes it is easier to live this kind of inauthentic life with other Christians who are walking with God. However, we must seek to be real and not be defensive in our relationships. We can trust God to help us make the following statements a reality in our lives:

- I will be known for who I really am.
- I will abandon all practices of self-justification, deceit, defensiveness, dodging, and manipulation.
- I will not give my life to public approval and "looking good."
- I will let my "yes" be "yes" and my "no" be "no." I will not speak out of both sides of my mouth. I will be known as a person who speaks the whole truth and tells it in love (see Ephesians 4:15).

GENUINE LOVE DOMINATES

The third element involved in transforming our social world is to let genuine love dominate our social lives. This means that pretenses will vanish from our lives. Pretense is pretending or playing "make-believe." It is an attitude that tries to look right on the outside but is insincere on the inside. I don't mean to make this kind of love sound easy—in a sense we must learn this lesson again and again all our lives—but increasingly, our love must be genuine.

The best overall description of the qualities that make up a community dominated by genuine love is found in Romans 12:9-21. I suggest that you take a moment now to read this out loud with your family or friends. I recommend this because it is one thing for you to make a commitment to love as an individual—and you should. However, this really works best when we experience it in Christian community with others who have made this same commitment in Christ. When nonbelievers see this kind of community, it can draw them like nothing else to Christ and His extended offer to join His family.

PAY IT FORWARD

The final action step is to "pay it forward." You may be familiar with the movie by that title. For Christians, this thought takes on an even deeper meaning. What Christ has done for us by dying on the cross—forgiving us of our attacks on and withdrawal from God—is impossible to pay back. What Christ invites us to do with our new lives is to "pay it forward." Christ wants us to love each other. Now that we are freed from defending and securing ourselves, we can devote our lives to the service of others. Through Christ, our lives can be focused on blessing others, particularly those closest to us, beginning with our family members and then moving out to others.

TAKE ACTION: Discuss with your group a "pay it forward" plan you could do for a person or a group of people. You might choose to do this activity with your group or individually.

This is possible only through the power of God within us. We cannot be the husband, wife, parent, sibling, or friend that God intends except in the power of God. Spiritual formation in Christ requires that we be happily reconciled to living in the hand of God and led by the hand of God. Though it is no guarantee of perfection, this relationship with God sets the stage for what will work best in our relationships with other people in our lives. Jesus gave us access to this wisdom in His teachings, and He showed us what it looks like by His own life.

Just think what our lives might be like if everyone reading these words—including those in your circle of sufficiency—actually captured the vision and intended to do these four things in the power of God. No more attacks. No more withdrawal. Instead, we'd be serving and blessing each other in the love that flows from our relationships with the triune God.

GROUP PRAYER: *O God, we want to love from the center of our lives, and we intend to start doing what it takes today! We have chosen new life through Christ, and we want to become authentic Christians living in authentic community. We will not pretend to be like Christ, but we will truly love with genuine love. And we will devote our lives to serving and blessing others just as Christ has served and blessed us. Help us to love others in Your power as You transform our social lives.*

WRAP UP

Let's review the principles from chapters 23 and 24.

CHAPTER 23: THE VISION TO TRANSFORM MY SOCIAL LIFE

In this chapter, we looked at four main points to consider as we seek to transform our social lives:

1. The Circle of Sufficiency
2. Two Actions That Wreck Our Relationships: Attack and Withdrawal
3. Reclaiming Community Through Trinitarian Love
4. The Place to Begin: The Family

CHAPTER 24: THE MEANS TO TRANSFORM MY SOCIAL LIFE

In this chapter, we looked at four means to achieve this vision:

1. Receive Your New ID in Christ
2. Lose the Mask
3. Genuine Love Dominates
4. Pay It Forward

MY PERSONAL PLAN FOR RENOVATING MY SOCIAL LIFE

I, _____, have embraced God's vision to transform my social life and intend to accomplish this vision through the following means (*put a check in each box that you intend to include as a part of your personal plan*):

❑ I will receive my new ID in Christ. (Make your own "Student ID" by photocopying the one on the following page or making your own from scratch; go to a local copy center and get it laminated.)

STUDENT ID IN CHRIST

Name:

"My life in Christ is whole and blessed, no matter what has or has not been done to me and no matter how shamefully my human circles of sufficiency have been violated."

Date of Spiritual Birth:

_____

INSERT PICTURE

❑ I will choose to lose the mask. (Consider personalizing the following points in your journal; ask yourself how your relationships are going in light of these commitments.)

  ○ I will be known for who I really am.

  ○ I will abandon all practices of self-justification, deceit, defensiveness, dodging, and manipulation.

  ○ I will not give my life to public approval and "looking good."

  ○ I will let my "yes" be "yes" and my "no" be "no." I will not speak out of both sides of my mouth. I will be known as a person who speaks the whole truth and tells it in love (see Ephesians 4:15).

❑ I will choose to let genuine love dominate my relationships. (Consider copying the covenant that follows and having your family or a group of friends read it, agree to it, and sign it. Place the covenant in a prominent place, such as on your refrigerator.)

COVENANT OF A FAMILY DOMINATED BY GENUINE LOVE

We will . . .

. . . love from the center of who we are; we won't fake it.

. . . run for dear life from evil and hold on for dear life to good.

. . . be good friends who love deeply.

. . . practice playing second fiddle.

. . . not quit in hard times but pray all the harder.

. . . help needy Christians.

. . . be inventive in hospitality.

. . . bless our enemies rather than cursing under our breath.

. . . laugh with each other when one of us is happy.

. . . share tears when one of us is down.

. . . get along with each other.

. . . not be stuck-up.

. . . make friends with nobodies.

. . . not be the great somebody.

. . . not hit back.

. . . discover the beauty in everyone.

. . . not insist on getting even; that's God's job.

(Adapted from Romans 12:9-21)

Everyone who agrees to this signs below:

_____   _____

_____   _____

_____   _____

❑ I will pay forward what Christ has done for me by serving others. (Use the covenant to accomplish this task; consider journaling your experiences.)

GROUP PRAYER: *Loving God, we have clearly seen Your vision for the transformation of our social lives. We give You our circles of community, and we intend to let You work in us to heal all of the broken parts of our circles. We will accomplish this healing and transformation by committing to our personal renovation plans. We will look to You each day to help us let genuine love dominate our relationships with You and with others. We love You!*

PART 10
TRANSFORMING
MY SOUL

*Only give heed to yourself and keep your soul diligently, so
that you do not forget the things which your eyes have seen.
(Deuteronomy 4:9, NASB)*

Throughout this book, we've been discussing the key elements of a
human being. But we live in this world as unified, living, breathing people.
This is where the soul comes in. At any given moment, the soul is what is
running your life. The soul is the whole you: heart, mind (thoughts and
feelings), body, and social life combined. It correlates, integrates, and
gives life to everything going on in the other four dimensions. It is the
life-center of the human being. In other words, your soul is in charge of
managing the other parts of you. It coordinates how each part responds
to the others.

Our souls are what respond to the events of our lives. For example,
if you find out that your best friend is moving to another state, it is
your soul that will respond to the news. Your mind will have thoughts
and feelings about this. Your heart will ultimately make a choice about
how you will respond. Your body will carry out that decision, whether
in hurt and withdrawal or hugs and tears. Ultimately, your friend's
move—a change that is outside your control—will affect your social
life because your best friend is in your circle of sufficiency. But your
soul is the integrating element that will conduct and present your
reaction.

Our souls are "deep." We can't fully get our arms around how they
work. They function almost totally beyond our conscious awareness.
Our souls are spiritual, or nonphysical. They have resources and relationships that exceed human comprehension, and they exist within an
infinite environment of which we have little knowledge. The Bible tells
us that we are "fearfully and wonderfully made" (Psalm 139:14, NIV).
When we think of how complex and even mysterious our souls are, it
can be just a little scary.

We do know this: God wants to transform the soul. Its renovation is absolutely critical if we desire to experience the best God offers in this life and the life to come. To move us in this direction, we will look in the next chapter at God's vision for renovating the soul and some of the obstacles that stand in the way. Then in chapter 26, we will turn our attention to the means for accomplishing the transformation of our souls.

What will it take to actually become like Christ in the depths of our souls? This section is going to require some definite work on your part to pull off this transformation. However, there is good news. God is there with you. It will be His grace that ultimately puts you in the winner's circle.

GROUP PRAYER: *Mighty God, we don't understand our souls. But we know that You do, for You created us with souls that conduct everything that goes on in our minds, hearts, bodies, and lives. We know that You want to transform our souls, so we ask that You will reveal Your vision of renovation to us. We want to become like Christ in the very deepest part of us—our souls—and we thank You for helping us to do it.*

CHAPTER 25

THE VISION TO TRANSFORM MY SOUL

As the deer pants for streams of water,
so my soul pants for you, O God.
My soul thirsts for God, for the living God.
(Psalm 42:1-2, NIV)

THE SOUL IS OUR ORGANIZER

Most people think of the soul as that immaterial and spiritual part of us that is contained in our bodies. Actually, the soul is bigger than that. The body is inside the soul, not vice versa. This may be hard for us to understand, but in a real sense we need to "think outside the box."

Here is an analogy from creation. Our solar system is made up of nine planets, each one a distinct part of the system. Yet as you look at each of the planets circling around the sun, it is hard to understand what holds them in place. There is no physical wall, and yet not one of them escapes. In this analogy, we might think of motion, gravity, and the complex centrifugal and centripetal forces at work as the "soul" that holds all nine planets in place. We could say that this "soul" is an invisible essence of our solar system. In a similar way, the individual parts of us—the heart, the mind's thoughts and feelings, the body, and our relationships—are like the planets. Each part is held together by the soul, a force in our lives that can't be seen but is very real nonetheless.

THINK IT THROUGH: Now that you're getting the gist of this soul thing, come up with your own analogy for the way the soul works together with the other four parts and share it with your group.

DEATH OF THE SOUL AND SOUL DENIAL

Because the study of the soul can be like nailing jelly to a wall, it has been very controversial among modern thinkers. Ultimately, many reject the idea of the soul because they find it hard to conclude that there is an enduring, nonphysical center that organizes life into a whole. As a result, most people who graduate from high school or college are not given a strong education on the reality and importance of the soul.

Think about this carefully. There are some very important aspects of our lives that are "soul functions"—they require the full participation of a healthy soul in order to work well. A few of these areas are creativity, sleep, sex, parenting, relationships, health, and meaningful work. Because modern intellectuals have dismissed the reality of the soul, it hasn't been fully developed in most people. Look again at the areas just mentioned and ponder how dysfunctional each of them has become in our time. One out of every two Americans over the age of eighteen struggles with some form of insomnia.[1] Sex has no boundaries in our society. Pornography is epidemic. Sexually transmitted diseases are spreading. The divorce rate is extremely high. Almost half of children today are being raised in a single-parent home.[2] And there is little sense of community.

So many people in our society are focused on themselves. The suicide rate among the elderly has never been higher; the reason cited is loneliness and the lack of a sense of belonging. Studies are showing that while teenagers have never been better off economically, they have never been worse off mentally, emotionally, or behaviorally.[3] Why should we be concerned about these issues? Because for each of these areas of life to work well, a fully functional soul is required.

The loss of the soul would explain why a sense of meaning is such a problem for people today. Meaning is one of the greatest needs of human life, one of our deepest hungers. Perhaps it is the most basic need in the realm of human experience. In the absence of meaning, boredom, aimless effort, and willpower are all that remain. Think about how you feel when you're studying for a final exam in a class whose value seems remote or minimal to you. Can you imagine feeling that way about your whole life?

In a life of boredom or "gutting it out" by mere willpower, almost nothing can be endured, and people who are well-off by other physical or social standards find such a life unbearable. They are "dead souls." By contrast, when we face a difficult assignment or task with a sense of meaning, there is a power beyond us that is exhilarating and sees us through. That is the presence of the soul.

Those who deny the soul through scientific reasoning still have to live life, and they need to find resources to do it. They still have to deal with life on *some* basis. What will that basis be? They find various ways, many of which continue to destroy or smother the soul.

But all of this is changing. There is a resurgence of thinkers today who recognize a need for change. They have grown weary of a world understood only in the physical sense and are probing the depths of issues surrounding the soul. They are making some fresh discoveries. If your generation continues to pursue this path and stays true to God's Word by looking at it deeply and carefully, you will participate in rediscovering the role of the soul. You will become a Psalm 1 person.

BE A PSALM 1 PERSON

> How well God must like you —
>> you don't hang out at Sin Saloon,
>> you don't slink along Dead-End Road,
>> you don't go to Smart-Mouth College.
> Instead you thrill to GOD's Word,
>> you chew on Scripture day and night.
> You're a tree replanted in Eden,
>> bearing fresh fruit every month,

Never dropping a leaf,
> *always in blossom.*
You're not at all like the wicked,
> *who are mere windblown dust—*
Without defense in court,
> *unfit company for innocent people.*
GOD *charts the road you take.*
> *The road they take is Skid Row. (Psalm 1)*

The man described in Psalm 1 is a "soul man." The renovation of the soul can come about only when we realize we do not know how to govern our souls. The "soul man" turns to the "soul book." The Bible—the laws of God—contains the secrets and directives for ordering our souls and growing them into Christlikeness. Followers of God know better than to trust their own wisdom. They turn to God. The person described in Psalm 1 exemplifies "soul living."

The person in the psalm is first characterized in terms of what he does *not* do, which is perhaps the most immediately obvious thing about him. He does not determine his course of action by the influence of those without God—even their latest brilliant ideas. He does not live as if God does not exist, nor does he make plans from a strictly human understanding. He plans on God (see verse 2).

The person who lives only within human wisdom will experience an inclination to do what is wrong. In contrast, the Psalm 1 person "thrills to GOD's Word" and therefore does not position himself to do wrong. He thrills in the law that God has given, the Bible—the real "Chicken Soup for the Soul." He loves it and can't keep his mind off of it. He thinks it is beautiful, strong, wise, and an incredible gift of God's mercy and grace. He therefore dwells upon it day and night, turning it over and over in his mind and speaking it to himself. He does not do this to please God but rather because the law pleases him. It is the North Star that orients his whole being.

The result is a flourishing life. The image used here is that of a tree planted by water canals. No matter what the weather or the surface condition of the ground, its roots go down into the water and bring up life. As a result, the tree bears fruit when it is supposed to, and its foliage is always bright with life. It prospers in what it does. Likewise the person who is rooted in God through His law: "Whatever he does prospers" (verse 3, NIV).

DON'T BE A ROMANS 1 PERSON

But God's angry displeasure erupts as acts of human mistrust and wrongdoing and lying accumulate, as people try to put a shroud over truth. But the basic reality of God is plain enough. Open your eyes and there it is! By taking a long and thoughtful look at what God has created, people have always been able to see what their eyes as such can't see: eternal power, for instance, and the mystery of his divine being. So nobody has a good excuse. What happened was this: People knew God perfectly well, but when they didn't treat him like God, refusing to worship him, they trivialized themselves into silliness and confusion so that there was neither sense nor direction left in their lives. They pretended to know it all, but were illiterate regarding life. They traded the glory of God who holds the whole world in his hands for cheap figurines you can buy at any roadside stand. . . .

Since they didn't bother to acknowledge God, God quit bothering them and let them run loose. And then all hell broke loose: rampant evil, grabbing and grasping, vicious backstabbing. They made life hell on earth with their envy, wanton killing, bickering, and cheating. Look at them: mean-spirited, venomous, fork-tongued God-bashers. Bullies, swaggerers, insufferable windbags! They keep

inventing new ways of wrecking lives. They ditch their parents when
they get in the way. Stupid, slimy, cruel, cold-blooded. And it's not
as if they don't know better. They know perfectly well they're spitting
in God's face. And they don't care—worse, they hand out prizes to
those who do the worst things best! (Romans 1:18-23,28-32)

For many people, living as a Psalm 1 person remains an impossible
dream, for their souls are running amuck and their lives are in chaos. By
default, they have given themselves to being Romans 1 people. They
have given their lives to their bodily desires and habits (gossip, open
sexual participation, and sexual perversions). Blinded by false ideas
(for students, these come from pop culture through music, movies, and
television), they live by distorted images (such as dysfunctional families
as a norm) and misinformation (they simply don't have the truth of
God's Word). Because of this blindness, their souls cannot find their way
into a life of consistent truth and harmonious pursuit of what is good.
Their souls are locked in a self-destructive struggle internally and with
everything and everyone around them. Usually, unfulfilled desires and
poisonous relationships are the most prominent features of such lives.

We each have a "soul file." In that file are pieces of information
specific to our development in the other dimensions of our lives (you
could say this is *information* on our *formation* in each of the parts of our
lives). We have:

1. Mind's Thought File—Details on how we think about life
2. Mind's Feeling File—Details on how we feel about life
3. Body File—Details on bodily behavior
4. Heart File—Details on choices made
5. Social Relationship File—Details on how we handle relationships

The soul's job is to take this information (or formation) and interact
with it to live life. The problem is that the files do not guide the soul

in a unified direction. This means that most souls cannot produce an inner harmony, much less align with truth and with God. For example, what we believe in our minds' thoughts may not be consistent with how we treat people or use our bodies. Our habitual condition may be one of conflict, and our actions may be inconsistent with our intentions or what we regard as wise.

Here is another way of understanding the function of the soul. Let's say you serve on a jury with four other people, and you have been elected chairperson. You and the other jurors have to agree on whether or not a person is guilty of murder. Everyone on the jury thinks differently and hears the testimonies differently. Everyone has a different idea of what is right and what is wrong. Your job as the chairperson is to organize everyone on the jury to come to a unified decision based on the truth. If you can't eventually bring the jury members to a unified conclusion, the judge will declare your jury a hung jury. In the spiritual life, the soul is the chairperson, and the heart, the mind, the body, and the social life are the four members. When the members of our lives are not growing and working in harmony with each other, our souls struggle to bring our lives together. We can end up with a "hung life" if we're not immersed in God's Word.

The Psalm 1 person has a progressively healthy soul under God and is able to sort all this out so the other four parts live in harmony. He or she sees the need to transform every file, every jury member, every part. The Romans 1 person has a progressively unhealthy soul apart from God, and eventually God lets that person have his or her way—and the result is a ruined life.

A transformed soul does not permit a part of a person's life to be inconsistent or in disharmony with the other parts. The transformed soul is an ordered soul under the law of God. The dimensions of self (heart, thoughts, feelings, body, and social life) are coherently drawn together by the soul to form a whole life devoted to God and to what He says is good.

This is God's vision for the transformed soul. This is where God wants you to be!

GROUP PRAYER: *Father God, our souls are the essence of who we are. We see Your vision for transforming our souls, and we see that we must learn to love and live Your Word. We want our thoughts, feelings, behaviors, choices, and relationships to be ordered by Your law. We choose to renovate our souls by delighting ourselves in Your Word.*

CHAPTER 26

THE MEANS TO TRANSFORM MY SOUL

"Go stand at the crossroads and look around.
Ask for directions to the old road,
The tried and true road. Then take it.
Discover the right route for your souls." (Jeremiah 6:16)

VISION

God has a vision for transforming your soul. In the last chapter, we tried to get our arms around the big idea of the soul and its important role in organizing our lives into a whole. We realized that we must have God's master plan for renovating the dimensions of our lives—the heart, mind's thoughts and feelings, body, and social life. The soul relies heavily on the move toward godliness in each of these parts. For the soul to be strong and healthy so it can do its job of ordering our lives around God's wonderful law, we must give special attention to its own spiritual transformation. For this to become a reality, we must begin with vision. We must embrace God's vision as our vision to bring the soul under His reign.

INTENTION

By this point in the book, you should know that with a biblical vision must come biblical intent. We must intend or decide in our hearts to move in the direction of a biblical renovation of our souls. With vision and intent firmly in place, we will turn our attention to the means: four specific things that God expects you to do to experience the renovation of your soul.

MEANS

ACKNOWLEDGE YOUR SOUL AND PLACE IT UNDER GOD

The very first thing to do is to be mindful of your soul, to acknowledge it, and to place it under God. In spiritual transformation, it is necessary to take the soul seriously and deal with it regularly and intelligently. We must be sure to do this on our own and also in our Christian fellowships.

This might seem strange because most people think of the soul as already "religious." Secular culture dismisses it. Because there has been so little teaching on the soul in recent years in the Western world, it is important to first simply acknowledge the soul and its need to be renovated.

Some conservative and evangelical churches still sometimes talk about "saving" the soul. Perhaps this is what you were taught. Once the soul is "saved," it is usually treated as needing no further attention. Ignoring the soul is one reason Christian churches have become fertile sources of recruits for cults and other religious and political groups. It is unreasonable to think the soul would be properly cared for when it isn't even seriously acknowledged. This has to change. We must emphatically and repeatedly acknowledge the soul as the living center of the Christian life. Further, we must reassume the responsibility for the care of souls, a responsibility long assigned to us in Christian tradition. As individuals, we must "own" our souls and take responsibility before God for them, turning to our pastors, teachers, and parents for the necessary help.

YOKE YOURSELF TO CHRIST

Once we clearly acknowledge the soul (who we are as a whole), we can learn to hear our soul cries. Jesus heard soul cries from the weary humanity He saw around Him. He saw the soul's desperate need in those who struggled with the overwhelming tasks of their lives. Such weariness and endless labor was to Him a sure sign of souls not properly rooted in God—souls, in effect, on their own. He saw the multitudes around Him, and it tore His heart, for they were "distressed and dispirited like sheep without a shepherd" (Matthew 9:36, NASB). He invited such people to become His students by yoking themselves to Him and letting Him show them how He would pull their load (see Matthew 11:28-30).

WHAT IS A YOKE? A yoke is a wooden bar that fits over the necks of two oxen so they move in the same direction at the command of the farmer. Attached to the yoke may be an instrument that tills the earth or carries a load.

Being in Jesus' yoke is not a matter of taking on additional labor to crush us all the more. Rather, it is a matter of learning how to use His strength *and* ours together to bear our load *and* His. We will find His yoke an easy one and His burden light because in learning from Him, we learn to rest our souls in God. Our souls are at peace when they are with God, as a child is with its mother.

ABANDON OUTCOMES TO GOD THROUGH HUMILITY

One of the main things we learn when we yoke ourselves to Christ is to abandon outcomes to God. In this process, we accept our powerlessness—in our hearts, souls, minds, and strength—to make things come out the way we want.

GIVING IT TO GOD: Here is a list of possible outcomes that you may need to abandon to God:

- Dating the person you want
- Getting married
- Being popular
- Earning a lot of money
- Getting your parents back together
- Avoiding illness or disease

- Making the football team
- Getting voted to student council
- Getting accepted to the college of your choice

Can you think of others? Try to personalize this list with your group.

This doesn't mean that we shouldn't do practical things to make ourselves attractive to others, finish school to enhance our chances of making a good living, or exercise to stay healthy. It means that we should leave the outcome—and the worry that goes with it—to God.

To move our souls in this direction, Peter tells us, "Clothe yourselves with humility" (1 Peter 5:5, NIV). He goes on to say, "So be content with who you are, and don't put on airs. God's strong hand is on you; he'll promote you at the right time. Live carefree before God; he is most careful with you" (1 Peter 5:6-7). God has a plan for us that goes far beyond what we can work out on our own. We simply have to rest in Him as He reveals it to us.

Resting in God, we can be free from all anxiety, which means deep soul rest (see Philippians 4:6-7). We no longer fret or get angry when others seem to be doing better than we are, even though we may think they are less deserving.

On the other hand, an ongoing pattern of disobedience to what's right distances us from God. This way of life is rooted in pride. We think we are "big enough" to take our lives into our own hands and disobey, instead of humbling ourselves under God's almighty hand. We believe that if we don't take matters into our own hands, we will not get what we want. In contrast, a humble person who has abandoned outcomes to God takes this attitude: "There is no reason why I should get what I want because I am not in charge of the universe." The more we get to know God and His ways, the more we begin to live in the pattern of Psalm 37:4. As we delight ourselves in the Lord, the desires of our hearts will become more like His desires for us.

RECEIVE, STUDY, AND INTERNALIZE THE LAW OF GOD
TO THE POINT OF OBEDIENCE

The best place to turn for help to abandon outcomes to God—and resist abandoning God for our outcomes—is the Law of God. Many newcomers to the first five books of the Old Testament think they are nothing more than just a list of rules and commandments. But they are so much more. The Law provides us with a picture of reality—of how things are with God and His creation. When we add to the Law the other writings of the Bible, we are given vital insight that enables us to know God, what He is doing, and what we are to do. David said it best in Psalm 19:7:

> The law of the LORD is perfect,
> reviving the soul. (NIV)

The Bible contains everything we need to accomplish God's purposes. It is a road map to living out God's will.

Therefore, if we wish to transform our souls, we must lean on the law of God. We need to approach it with a grateful heart. We need to receive it, study it, and internalize it to the point of obedience. We need to actually do what it says (see James 1:22).

This does not mean that we can simply read the Bible and obey it as an act of total human effort. We have already established that God is present in the lives of His followers through faith in Jesus Christ. The grace and power that He extends to us to justify us before God (establish the relationship) is the same grace and power He extends to us to sanctify the relationship (grow the relationship). We must also remember that the Bible is not an ordinary book. We read in Hebrews that "the word of God is living and active. Sharper than any double-edged sword, it penetrates even to dividing soul and spirit, joints and marrow; it judges the thoughts and attitudes of the heart" (4:12, NIV). We do not study the law of God in our strength alone. We study and apply God's Word in His strength for it to be rightly applied in our lives. A person whose aim is anything less than obedience to the law of God in the Spirit and power of Jesus will never have a soul at rest in God. And that person will never advance significantly in spiritual formation into Christlikeness.

In this chapter, we have laid out four specific means to accomplish the vision God intends for the transformation of our souls. They are:

1. Acknowledge your soul and place it under God.
2. Yoke yourself to Christ.
3. Abandon outcomes to God through humility.
4. Receive, study, and internalize the law of God to the point of obedience.

Each of these action steps builds on the one before. You cannot move forward on the second until you have accomplished the first, and so on. Careful consideration and application of these points will definitely draw you closer to God. You will move forward in your quest to become a fully devoted and transformed follower of Jesus.

GROUP PRAYER: *Holy God, we embrace Your vision of bringing our souls under Your reign, and we intend to move toward a biblical renovation of our souls. We know our souls are our centers, and we will learn to take care of them by yoking ourselves to Christ. We will learn to rest in You and will devote ourselves to listening to, studying, and internalizing Your Word. We will learn to do what Your Word says so that we can become like Christ.*

WRAP UP

Let's review the principles from chapters 25 and 26.

CHAPTER 25: THE VISION TO TRANSFORM MY SOUL

- The Soul Is Our Organizer
- Death of the Soul and Soul Denial
- Be a Psalm 1 Person
- Don't Be a Romans 1 Person

CHAPTER 26: THE MEANS TO TRANSFORM MY SOUL

- Acknowledge Your Soul and Place It Under God
- Yoke Yourself to Christ
- Abandon Outcomes to God Through Humility
- Receive, Study, and Internalize the Law of God to the Point of Obedience

MY PERSONAL PLAN FOR RENOVATING MY SOUL

I, _____, have embraced God's vision to transform my soul and intend to accomplish this vision through the following means (*put a check in each box that you intend to include as a part of your personal plan*):

❑   I will acknowledge my soul and place it under God.

　　o   I will emphatically and repeatedly acknowledge my soul as the living center of my Christian life, place it under God, and assume responsibility for its care.

　　o   I will memorize and meditate on Psalm 42:1-2:

> *As the deer pants for streams of water,*
> *so my soul pants for you, O God.*
> *My soul thirsts for God, for the living God. (NIV)*

❑ I will yoke myself to Christ.

    o I am committed to learning how to handle life the way Christ handles it.

    o I will memorize and meditate on Matthew 11:28-30:

> *"Come to me, all you who are weary and burdened, and I will give you rest. Take my yoke upon you and learn from me, for I am gentle and humble in heart, and you will find rest for your souls. For my yoke is easy and my burden is light."* (NIV)

❑ I will abandon outcomes to God through humility.

    o I will memorize and meditate on 1 Peter 5:6-7:

> *So be content with who you are, and don't put on airs. God's strong hand is on you; he'll promote you at the right time. Live carefree before God; he is most careful with you.*

    o I will make a list of outcomes I am really counting on. Next, I will write out a prayer to God turning over these outcomes to Him. I will tell Him that I trust in Him and know that His plans are good.

    o Every time I encounter one of these issues in my life, I will whisper a short prayer to God, saying, "I abandon the outcome to You, O Lord."

❑ I will receive, study, and internalize the law of God to the point of obedience.

    o I am committed to being a Psalm 1 person instead of a Romans 1 person. I will read Psalm 1 and Romans 1:18-23,28-32 every day for one week. At the end of each reading, I will offer a prayer of commitment to God to be a Psalm 1 person with His help.

o I will do a personal study of Psalm 119.

o I will read through the five books of the Law (the first five books of the Bible). A good resource is *The Message Remix* by Eugene H. Peterson. See www.NavPress.com.

o I will make a commitment to read through the Bible in a year. (There are many reading plans that will help you accomplish this. Check out this website for some examples: http://www.navpress.com/Magazines/DJ/BibleReadingPlans.asp. Try to do it in a year, but don't give up if it takes you two years. Let the readings run through your soul. Commit each reading time to God in prayer.)

GROUP PRAYER: *Dear God, we don't want to have dead souls, and so we acknowledge that our souls are the very center of our lives. We commit to our personal renovation plans so that we can have truly renovated souls. We will take care of our souls, and we will rest in You. We will trust You to take care of the outcomes in our lives, and we will be humble. And we will commit ourselves to Your Word so that we can become Psalm 1 people. Renovate our souls, God!*

THINK AGAIN

Now it is time to look back and to look forward: back to what we have studied in this book and forward to our lives—to what lies ahead of us—because we are becoming the persons we will be for eternity.

At the beginning of this book, you looked at your vision for your life. The question has now shifted: "What is *God's* vision for your life?" That is the all-important question and the one we have attempted to uncover in these pages.

We have searched out the path of spiritual formation as seen in the followers of Jesus Christ through the ages. The renovation of the heart in Christlikeness is not something that concerns the heart alone. The heart cannot be renovated if the other parts of our lives remain in the grip of evil. Willpower is not the key to personal transformation. Rather, the will and character only progress as *all other parts of us* come into line with the intent of a will brought to newness of life "from above" by the Word and the Spirit.

The full renovation project also includes our minds' thoughts and feelings, our bodies, our social lives, and our souls. God calls us as His followers to devote our lives to putting on the character of Christ. Hebrews 12:1 calls this pursuit "the race marked out for us" (NIV).

How we run this race is very important. As we run, we seek to avoid getting tangled up in sin. Of course, we work at being patient with ourselves. We take a long view of the race that is set before us. It is a marathon. We don't try to accomplish everything at once, and we don't try to force things. If we don't immediately succeed in removing a weight or sin, we just keep running—steadily, patiently—while we find out how it can be removed in God's way (see Hebrews 12:1).

As we run this race, we need to keep looking up at our Coach, who gave us faith to run in the first place and who will bring us safely to the end. We concentrate on His thoughts, feelings, character, body, social being, and soul. We constantly learn from Him, and He shows us how to let the weights and sins drop off so we can run better (see Hebrews 12:2).

As we run, we sense divine assistance making our steps lighter. We realize truth more strongly and see things more clearly. We find greater joy in those running with us—our companions in Christ—as well as those who went before us and those coming after.

If you have followed the overall intent of this book, you should have a detailed and doable plan to run this worthy race. I pray that you will run the race Christ set before you. I pray that you have set your will to this task. I pray that you will have a family, a community, a band of brothers and sisters in Christ who will run the race with you.

This world is aching for people who take Jesus at the power of His word and seek to become the kind of people He envisioned them to be. For the people who have been divinely appointed to be in your life, you need to be Jesus to them. You are not called to judge them but to serve them as best you can by the light you have.

Whatever your situation, now is the time to make the changes and undertake the initiatives that are indicated by the lessons we have studied in this book. I leave you with the inspiring words of Paul: "There has never been the slightest doubt in my mind that the God who started this great work in you would keep at it and bring it to a flourishing finish on the very day Christ Jesus appears" (Philippians 1:6).

GROUP PRAYER: *Oh dear God, we want to have renovated hearts, and we have seen Your vision for our lives. We give You our thoughts, our feelings, our hearts, our bodies, our social lives, and our souls for Your renovation. We* *will run the race You have set before us, and we will keep our eyes on Jesus Christ, who will keep us running until the end. We thank You for giving us the means to carry out Your vision, and we commit to finishing strong for You! Thank You for Your renovating work in us.*

NOTES

HOW TO USE THIS BOOK
1. Quentin J. Schultze and others, *Dancing in the Dark: Youth, Popular Culture and the Electronic Media* (Grand Rapids, Mich.: Eerdmans, 1990), p. 240.

WELCOME TO THE GREATEST ADVENTURE OF YOUR LIFE
1. *The Matrix*, ©Warner Bros., Inc. All rights reserved.

CHAPTER 1: LESSON 1
1. *Merriam-Webster's Collegiate Dictionary*, 11th ed., s.v. "Revolution."

CHAPTER 2: LESSONS 2–4
1. *Merriam-Webster's Collegiate Dictionary*, 11th ed., s.v. "Science."

CHAPTER 4: DEFINING THE PARTS OF ME, PART 1
1. Thomas Camilli, *A Case of Red Herrings: Solving Mysteries Through Critical Questioning, Book A1* (Pacific Grove, Calif.: Critical Thinking Books & Software, 1992), p. 7.
2. Camilli, p. 33.

CHAPTER 9: SELF-DENIAL: THE PATH TO RADICAL GOODNESS, PART 1
1. John Calvin, *Institutes of the Christian Religion*, vol. 2 (Grand Rapids, Mich.: Eerdmans, 1975), p. 7.

CHAPTER 12: THE VISION TO BE A KINGDOM PERSON
1. Patricia Hersch, *A Tribe Apart* (New York: Ballantine Books, 1998), p. 167.

CHAPTER 15: THE VISION TO TRANSFORM MY MIND'S THOUGHTS
1. Roland H. Bainton, *Here I Stand: A Life of Martin Luther* (New York: The New American Library, 1955), p. 144.

CHAPTER 19: THE VISION TO TRANSFORM MY HEART
1. Andrew Murray, *Absolute Surrender* (Chicago: Moody, n.d.), p. 124. Murray was born in South Africa in 1828. After receiving his education in Scotland and Holland, he spent many years in Africa as both a pastor and missionary. He wrote some of the most enduring classics of Christian devotional literature.

2. An advocate of peace and lover of all creation, Saint Francis of Assisi lived from 1181 to 1226 and is the patron saint of animals and the environment. He founded the Franciscan Order.
3. Richard J. Foster, *Prayers from the Heart* (San Francisco: HarperSanFranciso, 1994), p. 107.

CHAPTER 23: THE VISION TO TRANSFORM MY SOCIAL LIFE
1. *Merriam-Webster's Collegiate Dictionary*, 11th ed., s.v. "Sufficient."

CHAPTER 25: THE VISION TO TRANSFORM MY SOUL
1. Archibald D. Hart, *The Anxiety Cure* (Nashville: W Publishing, 1999), p. 193.
2. The Commission on Children at Risk, *Hardwired to Connect: The New Scientific Case for Authoritative Communities* (YMCA of the USA, Dartmouth Medical School, and the Institute for American Values, 2003), p. 9.
3. The Commission on Children at Risk, p. 8.

ABOUT THE AUTHORS

DALLAS WILLARD is a professor in the School of Philosophy at the University of Southern California. He is the author of several books, including *Renovation of the Heart* and *Christianity Today*'s Book of the Year in 1999, *The Divine Conspiracy*. Dallas and his wife live in California.

RANDY FRAZEE is senior pastor of Pantego Bible Church in Fort Worth, Texas, a church known for its work in spiritual formation and community. He's the author of *The Connecting Church, Making Room for Life*, and *The Christian Life Profile Assessment Tool*.

SPIRITUALIZE EVERYTHING YOU DO.

Greater Than

Forge a faith that doesn't flinch amid the mysteries of the Father. Forty story-driven meditations invite students to wrestle with all that God is and to set off in pursuit of a God who is more than a little dangerous.
Mark Tabb   1-57683-606-1

Praise Habit

David Crowder redefines your perspective of a God beyond imagination and helps you develop a habit of praising Him by reflecting on targeted psalms from *The Message Remix.*
David Crowder   1-57683-670-3

Ask Me Anything

Dr. Budziszewski (aka Professor Theophilus) offers his expert opinion to help you achieve personal insight about the most controversial and confusing topics of our time.
J. Budziszewski   1-57683-650-9

To order copies, visit your local Christian bookstore,
call NavPress at 1-800-366-7788, or log on to www.navpress.com.

To locate a Christian bookstore near you,
call 1-800-991-7747.

NAVPRESS ®
BRINGING TRUTH TO LIFE
www.navpress.com